RUFINO TAMAYO

RUFINO TAMAYO

BY EMILY GENAUER

**HARRY N. ABRAMS, INC.
PUBLISHERS, NEW YORK**

1. Frontispiece. WOMAN IN ECSTASY.
1973. $51\frac{3}{8} \times 76\frac{5}{8}''$.
Harry N. Abrams Family Collection

JOHN L. HOCHMANN, *Executive Editor*
MARGARET L. KAPLAN, *Managing Editor*
NAI Y. CHANG, *Creative Director*
THERESA BRAKELEY, ANN L. GOEDDE, *Editors*
GAIL ASH, *Book Design*
BARBARA LYONS, *Picture Editor*

Library of Congress Cataloging in Publication Data

Genauer, Emily, 1911–
    Rufino Tamayo.

    Bibliography: p.
    1. Tamayo, Rufino, 1899–   I. Tamayo, Rufino,
1899–
ND259.T3G4   759.972   74–2150
ISBN 0-8109-0500-0

CONTENTS

LIST OF PLATES

*Colorplates are marked with an asterisk**

RUFINO TAMAYO

"An artist is only an artist on condition that he...neglect no aspect of his dual nature," wrote Baudelaire, concluding a long essay examining the phenomenon of creativity.[1]

The dualities in the art, thought, and temperament of Rufino Tamayo come quickly to mind. His pictures are at once sophisticated and childlike, sensuous and austere, immobile and dynamic, violent and melancholy, concerned and stoic. More than in the case of most other artists, duality, indeed multiplicity, marks even his place in the hierarchy of world art, as well as the course of his development.

In his native Mexico Tamayo is widely regarded as the most brilliant of that country's twentieth-century painters.

In Europe an increasing number of critics, scholars, and collectors set him in that very small company (along with Picasso, Chagall, Henry Moore, Miró, Lipchitz, Calder) of the most gifted and innovative of the modern masters who lived into the last decade. It is a position buttressed by a long list of international art prizes and honors that have come to him.

However, in the United States, where Tamayo lived and worked intermittently for years, he is less familiar, at least to the general public, than a score of much younger artists who came on the scene riding successive waves of new aesthetic ideas that are already receding.

And that is as astonishing as it is unwarranted, because Tamayo is, indeed, much more than he is accounted by any of the three groups cited. Now in his seventy-sixth year, Tamayo stands as one of a handful of great masters our century has produced. His reputation will not live primarily as that of a tireless, energy-charged, endlessly inventive and generative experimenter (like Picasso); or a man whose own idiom, early arrived at, was so completely idiosyncratic as to constitute a greatly

[1] Charles Baudelaire, "De l'essence de rire," quoted in Edgar Wind, *Art and Anarchy*, Alfred A. Knopf, 1964, p. 26.

refreshing but isolated eddy flowing off the mainstream of art (like Chagall); or one whose major contribution may be counted a productive exploration or extension of technical means (like Braque). He is, rather, all of these—and more. His energy is prodigious; his style is as personal and inimitable as anyone's; his technical innovations are as constant and arresting. It is in what these qualities add up to that Tamayo's work is extraordinary—that is, a profound humanism, a moral fervor, almost lost in the art of our time.

But it is expressed in images, symbols, colors, textures that are the language of a poet, not of a teacher or a preacher. Tamayo exhorts, he exorcises, but he never declaims. His anger is not charged by a single horrifying episode in history which he makes the theme of a single work or group of works, and then disgorges. It is, in fact, not so much anger that he projects as a deep and constant disquietude, stirred by the realities of our time but expressed in pictures that are timeless in their lyrical imagery, their symbolism, and their sense of magic and mystery.

The dualism—Baudelaire himself defined it as "the power of being oneself and someone else at one and the same time"—goes further and deeper than a mere listing of the obvious polarities in Tamayo's pictures can indicate. He is a traditionalist in that he works according to ancient traditions of what an artist and his role are, yet he holds to no traditions in his actual images. His basic approach to composition is traditional; each of his pictures must be a well-made object, the outcome of a carefully calculated and executed plan. Yet the spill of his rich color, the opulence of his textures, the seemingly capricious course of his line, the sudden stabs of brightness, suggest spontaneity to the point of improvisation and even accident.

He began his career aiming to express his lyrical impulses and his observations of everyday life in a personal, original, temperate idiom forged out of the timeless formal language of art. But for some years now many of his best paintings have been demonic, impassioned expressions dealing with the plight of man in our time. These "statements" might, indeed, be considered doubly paradoxical, since they come so close to enigmatic abstraction as to resist easy reading in any literal or direct sense. A viewer may see them as sensuous, glowing aggregates of

12

materials, shapes, and colors. Yet their vibrations of darkness and terror are never very far below the surface.

Tamayo has been painting for over a half century, and in that time his pictures have changed completely in essence, mood, aim, impact, and form. But careful examination of them in chronological sequence reveals that to an astonishing degree his development has been in a direct, continuing, sustained line, and that certain small but striking identical technical devices keep recurring in early and late pictures alike.

There are other dualities in Tamayo that he has not, to go back for a moment to Baudelaire's precept, neglected. Although he is an enormously sophisticated man in temperament, experience, enthusiasms, associations, and life style, his deepest affinity is for the primitive culture of his Zapotec Indian ancestors, rather than for the art of his contemporaries, which he regards with respectful detachment.

He is an intensely sensitive man who quickly turns mocking, a gracious, gentle man who on occasion becomes sullen. He has a wit whose sharpness—sometimes cruelty—is generally sheathed in a singular and disarming charm and grace. He is a strong-minded, uncompromising man who has, nevertheless, yielded on what would seem to be an important aesthetic issue merely in the interests of domestic peace. Although he is profoundly concerned with the human body—there are relatively few Tamayo canvases in which it does not figure—he never works with nude female models. This is a conjugally imposed limitation which may actually have proved a spur to invention. His figures have a flayed, corroded, vibrating look conveying not only a sense of humanity deeper than that which proceeds from the image of flesh alone but also, on occasion, intimations of intensely erotic force. Yet at the same time, they are so spare that they offer no interference with the bold, pervasive, often bristling, scythelike, linear rhythms of many of his compositions.

Perhaps the contrasts instinct in Tamayo's temperament and his art, the surprise responses of which he is capable, the oblique and even perverse vision which enables him to transform a familiar image into something utterly and incongruously different and, thereafter, inescapably his own, may best be savored through examination of a single instance among many.

13

The Museum of Modern Art in New York City owns one of his best and most characteristic paintings of the period in the forties when he first moved away from agreeable still lifes of tropical fruits and figure studies of still and stately women to explore what might be called areas of anger and pain (plate 2). It depicts two fierce, baying dogs, their jaws open, their teeth bared, their straining bodies speaking the essence of animal fury. The picture has become famous, not only for its formal power but also as a symbol of the mindless, bestial contention rampant in the world. Tamayo meant it to be that, but he laughs when he recalls its origin. As early as 1934 he began to amuse himself with variations on themes and images he found in the popular art of Mexico, particularly advertising signs. His preoccupation was very similar to that of New York's Pop artists thirty years later. On a Mexico City billboard he saw a sign in which the strength of a pair of work pants was attested to by two dogs, each with a pants leg in his mouth, vainly pulling at a garment

2. *Animals.* 1941. 30⅛ × 40″.
Museum of Modern Art, New York.
Inter-American Fund

14

that remained intact. Tamayo saw the banal, comic image sardonically and transformed it into a shatteringly tragic universal one, totally his own.

For all his great acclaim in Mexico, Tamayo's position even there involves paradoxes. Mexican painting has been described by that country's distinguished poet Octavio Paz as "like all our contemporary arts—perhaps more clearly than the others—the result of the Mexican Revolution," which he then goes on to characterize as "an immersion of Mexico in its own being." Obviously Paz, who is Tamayo's friend, had in mind something far deeper than the revolution as historical fact offering artists inspiration, opportunity, and theme. He speaks explicitly of a breaking up of the forms—of social and political thought and practice as well as of art—which had hampered and, he says, "denaturalized" the country with historical superstitions.

Nevertheless, Mexico's political revolution of 1910 did serve as the specific instrument, some ten years later, for effecting what has been called an art revolution and was certainly an art renaissance, in some ways as significant, if relatively short-lived, in its impact as the Renaissance in Italian art had been five centuries earlier. It was responsible for the inauguration of a vast and daring mural painting program conceived to help promote, consolidate, and celebrate the objectives and achievements of the political revolution. One of the painters involved in it, Jean Charlot, described that program as "a mouthpiece for collective feelings, which, at the time, ran their gamut from the passionate mayhem of active revolution to the stilled depths of meditation that precede and follow action wherever Indian blood is concerned."[2]

The project saw the walls of public buildings all over the then still largely primitive country covered with heroic, narrative, and allegorical paintings designed to depict the extraordinary native cultural achievements before the arrival of the Spaniards, to narrate the tragic sacking of Pre-Columbian civilization not only by the Spaniards but also by succeeding onslaughts of foreign and even homegrown exploiters, and to instill in the people a new nationalism and a soaring faith in their future (plate 3).

Born in 1899, Tamayo was old enough to have participated even

---

[2] Alma Reed, *The Mexican Muralists*, Crown, New York, 1960, p. 26.

in the relatively early days of the mural program, alongside his senior colleagues, Diego Rivera, who was born in 1886, and José Clemente Orozco, born in 1883. Years passed, in any case, before the movement lost its momentum. David Siqueiros, only a year older than Tamayo, early joined Rivera and Orozco in what would become a world-famous trinity of Mexican muralists. Of the three, only Orozco's position still remains secure. The reputations of Rivera, Siqueiros, and others (among them Jean Charlot and Roberto Montenegro) who won rapid, enormous, and even international renown for their role in the mural program have slipped into a sharp decline. They are seen today as greatly gifted but bombastic, illustrative, rhetorical painters, more energetic than truly creative.

Tamayo's star, however, has risen steadily. This, too, as it relates to both his present position and the altered character of his art, may be seen as a contradiction. He missed out on early fame because of the already mentioned basic concern in his youth with art as a purely formal, lyrical expression, rather than as a vehicle for didactic statement. This is by no means to say that Tamayo was ideologically less involved with the struggle than were the artists who set out to paint it. It is, rather, to underscore that his aesthetic bent precluded his youthful participation in a state-sponsored mural program which inflamed national pride among the Mexican people, excited the imagination of that large part of the watching world aware of and fascinated by the extraordinary role assigned to art by the new government, and brought world renown to the major artists assigned to paint the murals.

It might be pointed out that among them were highly sophisticated painters—most notably Diego Rivera—who, while traveling or studying in Paris, had been exposed to or even played a role in the aesthetic revolution taking place in Europe during the century's first two decades. Apparently they had no compunctions against bringing their skills to the government's propaganda project in the most direct, narrative way. But they were not, as happened in Russia after its own political revolution, pressured to do so. Instead, they were permitted to pursue whatever aesthetic course they liked. Most of Mexico's artists either had, in fact, participated in the fighting or were, in any case, totally sympa-

thetic to the revolution. Tamayo was among the latter.

Tamayo's art, it might be said, was more profoundly affected by the revolution than that of any of the other artists. His own conviction was that the victorious struggle for freedom could better be celebrated and national pride nurtured by an art that, instead of grandiloquently recording the facts of the struggle, tried to express the new pride in the fusion of Indian and Spanish blood and culture which victory had generated. This was the "immersion of Mexico in its own being" which Octavio Paz described as the real revolution. And it led Tamayo, eventually, to that intense and never-ending study of and identification with Mexican Pre-Columbian art which has been the most significant and constant influence on his painting.

Here is how Tamayo recalls that early time and his own feeling about what was happening:

> Outside of Orozco, who never traveled, most of the artists involved on the mural projects had studied or worked in Paris for years. When they returned, because of the revolution, they and those of us at home were all trying to liberate ourselves politically and economically. In that atmosphere the artists turned strongly nationalist. At that moment it was *necessary* for us to be very nationalist. That meant we could go back to our roots and absorb from them whatever we could. We had to become sure of ourselves. Before the revolution the Mexican government didn't really believe in Mexico's artists. They thought that because we had no experience we knew nothing, and therefore anything of quality could come only from foreigners.
>
> The trouble was that the painters portrayed only a surface nationalism. They painted the facts of Mexico's history and culture, all leading to the facts of the revolution. But revolution is not a Mexican phenomenon. It happens all over the world. I'm not opposed in theory to what they did. It was natural for them. But I myself felt something beyond that. I was a rebel, not against the revolution, but against the Mexican mural

movement which was conceived to celebrate it. It is impossible, I feel, in this time when communications are so open, to set out deliberately to make an art which is Mexican, or American, or Chinese, or Russian. I think in terms of universality. Art is a way of expression that has to be understood by everybody, everywhere. It grows out of the earth, the texture of our lives and our experiences. Maybe it was because the other painters were older than I that they were so concerned with the facts of the revolution. I wanted only to go back to our roots, our wonderful plastic tradition. The others were not concerned about this. [This and subsequent direct quotations from Tamayo come from taped interviews of the author with the artist in his studio at Cuernavaca and in Mexico City.]

Actually the revolution did more than stimulate in Tamayo an ideological and spiritual identification with ancient Indian art and artifacts. It also made possible his physical exposure to them to such an extent that not only their essence but their forms left an ineradicable mark on his own art. The new government, as part of its campaign to foster national pride, instituted a program designed to familiarize Mexican craftsmen with the skill and inventiveness of traditional Indian folk arts. Tamayo, employed by the government as a teacher on that program, had his office on the premises of Mexico City's Museum of Anthropology.

The change in the spirit and forms of Tamayo's art wrought by the revolution did not occur immediately. Some ten years passed before it would be clearly visible. In the meantime, because of his abiding concern with picture making for its own sake, he chose not to be part of the project for painting the blatant propaganda murals on which his older colleagues were engaged. Instead, he continued to paint his luscious fruit still lifes and his compositions of musicians and of placid, heavy-limbed women. They were modest but deeply personal works, their emphasis on sometimes glowing, sometimes somber color, on texture, and on controlled and rhythmic design. They were competent, agreeable, and vital, and at any other time they might have won a large public

in Mexico (as they did subsequently in the United States)—not, however, when the country was being covered with huge, dramatic, exhortative murals proclaiming the country's rich but tragic past and glorious future, and when the galvanized artists of the world, as well as a good part of the art public, were absorbedly watching.

Yet Tamayo, who in his youth was out of the mainstream of art in Mexico because of his resistance to painting with a social theme, feels very differently today. "The artist must," he says, "portray the moment in which he is living"—a statement which marks him as a nonconformist once again. He came to his new social awareness, and his intensely personal and original style for projecting it, in the early forties, shortly before the international art world experienced a new revolution of its own in the outburst of Abstract Expressionism. Then, suddenly, the broadest possible interest was focused on, and great reputations were quickly built by, artists totally unconcerned with either the social content with which Tamayo was increasingly preoccupied or the ordered structure always basic to his art. In time it became apparent that Abstract Expressionism, which had seemed the product of uncontrolled accidents of gesture and medium conveying emotional impact chiefly because of its spontaneity, might also have social significance as a symbol of the chaos of the postwar period. But once again Tamayo was an outsider, as Abstract Expressionism totally absorbed the attention of painters, the art establishment, and even the art-interested public around the world.

Subsequently the movement lost its stature as a seminal force, to be replaced by various new idioms, early among them Pop art. Exponents of this style did and still do project a "message," and in specific images, but the images are generally the unedited, raw, banal ones of the urban environment, deliberately duplicated by the artists on an enormous scale, so that their effectiveness as sardonic or pejorative commentary derives primarily from their depressing dimension. And once again Tamayo, working to express his social convictions in rich, painterly forms, stood apart, as, in fact, he stands apart from exponents of still another recent and interesting idiom, Minimalism. Its practitioners employ austerely geometric forms, large enough to be read as architecture and totally devoid of either specific or implied meaning. They

intend them to be beautiful, in Plato's words, "always and absolutely," as opposed to having the "beauty of living things."

Here, then, is the situation of Tamayo, self-isolated for the first fifteen years of his career from the painting style and movement which might have brought to him, as it did to his Mexican contemporaries, the attention of the world, and for the next thirty-five years from the continuing succession of styles that have catapulted art during that time into a degree of popular consciousness unmatched in history. Unflaggingly he has held to the conviction that his painting must grow out of the social realities of our time, and that it must be put together with unrelaxing formal control and deliberation and with technical resources as complex, opulent, and subtle as he can command. What is extraordinary, therefore, is that, swimming forever against prevailing currents, he has still been able to reach a very large, growing, extremely sophisticated, and profoundly admiring audience.

There will be occasion later for examining in detail the course Tamayo followed during those fifty years of going it alone (alone, that is, in the matter of his developing style; his life has been extremely rich in personal and professional associations). First might be considered the preoccupations of our time that he finds so obsessive. They are, in fact, those which have been absorbing and troubling artists everywhere, although it will be seen that few view them with the humanistic passion of Tamayo. Chiefly these preoccupations are science and technology, with all the aesthetic speculations, the challenge, and the terrors they have provoked. Most other artists agonizing over the specter of technology see in it a threat to the ancient notion of art as the embodiment of one man's intensely personal reaction to the visible—or his own invisible, interior—world in images that will be valued for their uniqueness and expressiveness and eventually treasured, they hope, on the walls of public or private collections. Today this traditional idea (no matter how untraditional the express form it may take) has been challenged by another concept, which, at its most extreme, sees art as the product (often in multiples) of electronics, computers, information machines, environmental systems, and new materials and processes, with results that are often transient, disposable, and perhaps even intangible.

20

3. José Clemente Orozco.
The Coming of Quetzalcoatl;
Pre-Columbian Golden Age;
The Departure of Quetzalcoatl.
1932–34. Mural.
Trustees of Dartmouth College,
Hanover, N.H.

Tamayo refuses to consider seriously as art a process such as the operation of ticker-tape machines (which some museums have exhibited as art objects—the "art" being the noisy mechanical activity itself, not the machines or their tangles of outpouring tape). He grants validity to art made of machine parts, or utilizing mechanized movement, or fabricated of machine-made materials. But his own concern is overwhelmingly with man. He phrases his concern without equivocation: "We are in a dangerous situation, and the danger is that man may be absorbed and destroyed by what he has created." The technology which has guided man to the moon, he says, could also be pushing him over the edge of our value system into a situation where reason, sensibility, and feeling all are sacrificed, and man becomes a kind of apparatus directed by electronics.

At the same time he makes clear his own feeling that dehumanization is not the inevitable consequence of such an eventuality. It is not a doom decreed by angry gods. Man has created it and man can control it. The danger is that, with it, he is easing himself into grim enslavement. The vibrations being produced by electronics are not reducing man to a machine, which has its own brute power, but to a helpless, quivering instrument powerless to move, to think, to feel. Those vibrations pervade every aspect of our environment. It is this image of man assaulted, says Tamayo, which is the tragedy of our time and, therefore, the recurrent theme of many of his paintings. He speaks of it slowly and haltingly, his dark face brooding and intense, his bright eyes grave.

21

This is a time of great realities, which is not to say that it is a time for realism, nor is it a time spurring scientific, mental, and aesthetic speculation. The fact is that science has provided us with enormous technological means, but these means should give form to new ideas. Instead, they threaten now to absorb man, instead of serving him. Technology, having been devised by man, doesn't have to lead to man's dehumanization. Yet it is doing just that, and this is reflected in our art. Art used to be, in the broadest sense, prophetic. I'm not thinking about specifics, like da Vinci and his designs for flying machines. I have in mind, rather, that art used to announce things that were about to happen. Picasso, for example, in his fragmented Cubism before World War I, was telling us something about a world that would very soon fall apart. The Abstract Expressionists after World War II were telling us about *people* who would fall apart, confronted by complex, devastating inner agonies and their loss of a sense of identity. But now science and technology are very far ahead of art, and many artists, especially young ones, are deeply disturbed by this knowledge that art has fallen behind. They believe they must find new ways of expression by which they can hitch themselves to technology. Painting, they insist, is therefore dead. I object to this in principle. Painting, we know, is a two-dimensional way of expression, and it cannot be anything else. I find some of the new experiments with new materials interesting, but I refuse to call them painting. Science and technology need not be dehumanizing at all. The fact is that man is creating all this. I'm praying that a new kind of humanism may emerge, in which man, harnessing the technology he has invented, lives more fully as a man.

In the meantime the artist has to portray the moment in which he is living. And for me this is a tragic moment, this time when man is assaulted by machines. I want to emphasize that the forms in my machines don't look like machines. They look like lifeless apparatus to which terrible things are done. I am painting the vibrations being produced by electronics in

man and his environment right now. I am thinking specifically about—but painting in metaphors—how man has permitted technological advances to pollute his natural resources; how they have required and made possible the construction of buildings of such scale that they block out our light and air and fence in our streets, and how they produce lethal weaponry. I'm haunted by the fear that technology will reduce men and women to robots and calculating machines, if it even lets them live at all.

Several of Mexico's major muralists also brought technology and even machines into their compositions. They viewed these devices, predictably, as indispensable elements in a developing program of industrialization which would determine the country's future through effecting the liberation of her peasants and promoting the self-sufficiency and enrichment of her national economy. Rivera, for instance, in his frescoes treated machinery in this literal and unimaginative way. Orozco's machines are abstracted so that they become a totemic demon, so to speak, devouring people caught in a capitalist system. Actually, many artists of every possible style and temperament in the twentieth century have directed themselves to the machine. The Italian Futurists, such as Balla and Severini, attempted before World War I to convey the power and dynamism of machines in stylized images of machine shapes. The Russian Constructivists after the war sought to emulate the precision and structure of machines in abstractions depicting or made with machine techniques and materials. Léger, in the twenties, stylized machine shapes into forms that yielded what were essentially still decorative Cubist paintings (plate 5). Alexander Calder used machines to power constructions that are still basically traditional in that they are sculptured objects, although invested with the additional element of movement, so that they physically animate the space they occupy instead of just displacing it.

A newer generation, taking its cue from Calder and perhaps most notably exemplified by the Swiss artist Jean Tinguely and the American Claes Oldenburg, is extending Calder's approach (plate 4). But instead of merely animating space with their machine-activated con-

4. Jean Tinguely. *M. K. III.*
1964. $36\frac{1}{4} \times 82\frac{1}{2}''$.
The Museum of Fine Arts, Houston.
Purchased from funds donated
by Dominique and John de Menil

structions, such artists offer the extra *frisson* of machines or machine parts ingeniously and wittily incorporated into their works to satirize machinery itself and our whole machine culture. Today a number of younger men feel that the idea of the artist's making pictures and sculptural objects at all is obsolete. Instead, they offer conceptions expressed through the most sophisticated of technological methods, producing no objects at all but presenting as aesthetic experience the processes of such inventions as laser beams, computer systems, sound synthesizers. Up to now their vision has rarely been shaped in any fundamental, organic way by the devices and innovations that advanced technology may offer artists. Their efforts have turned out to be, rather, visualizations in light and space of such earlier design concepts as were projected in drawings made by the Russian Constructivists over a half century ago.

While technology is clearly the concern of many artists today, Tamayo's feeling about it, as expressed in his paintings, could not be further removed from theirs. He is involved neither with machines as provocative or symbolic shapes nor with speculations about and experiments with new techniques and the materials that many artists feel as a tantalizing challenge. He sees technology, instead, in big, mythic terms, as an implacable, devastating force looming over men almost, one gathers, as he feels the gods loomed over ancient Mexico, where they were the source of light, energy, rain, fire—all the gifts men required to live—but also regularly demanded cruel blood sacrifices. Technology to him is the root of present-day man's great dilemma, the cause of his frailty and fear, but at the same time the instrument by which he can rise above himself and his present needs.

In many of his most striking pictures of recent years Tamayo has depicted that dilemma and consequent anguish. Instead of machines themselves, which appear in very few of his works, or even a symbolic specter representing mechanization, he paints a corrupted way of life in which the unseen machine is felt as a metaphoric instrument of our own greed and stupidity, the equivalent of primeval forces which have led in other periods to cataclysmic devastation. One is reminded, studying these paintings, of Plato's words in *The Republic:* "Teach me to rage correctly." Tamayo rages "correctly."

24

Tamayo's compositions are conceived with the utmost deliberation. He pares his figures down to constructions of cones, cylinders, and wedges, organized into great, swinging, somehow portentous rhythms, so that while they may lose virtually all their resemblance to human beings, their impact remains deeply, although enigmatically, human. Tamayo is not painting cadenced shapes and patterns. He is painting human figures seemingly skinned alive by a world they made themselves. Now, totally vulnerable, stripped of substance and flesh (as, literally, human beings were in some ritual sacrifices of ancient Mexico), they stand trembling and shaking like machines in a space charged with hostility. They wander moonstruck (surely Tamayo feels the moon as powerfully as the French Impressionists felt the sun), in a place of perpetual night and nameless terror, under skies alive with menacing labyrinths of nebulae about to explode. Sometimes they scream out like wounded, howling dogs. Sometimes they reach desperately to the stars. Sometimes they bellow in diabolic exultation.

All this would seem a moralistic message, instinct with the conviction—reinforced by Tamayo's own words—that man has a choice, that he can alter his course, redeem himself, eventually control his destiny. Yet he is painting no visible sermon but only what he suffers in that which he calls "this tragic moment in history."

Still, all moments in history have been tragic, going back to the bloody religious practices his Indian ancestors devised to placate their awesome gods. The Indians' exploitation and decimation by the conquistadores were no less calamitous. Terrified man has always been confronted by incomprehensible forces bigger, crueler, more powerful than himself. Aeschylus in "Prometheus Bound" describes a scene that might be a program note to one of Tamayo's typical paintings of a shattered, lonely, sticklike figure confronting the firmament—man isolated before some terrible force:

Savage winds convulse the sky
Hurricanes shake the earth from its foundations
The waves of the sea rise up and drown the stars. . . .[3]

5. Fernand Léger. *The Disks.*
1918–19. 94$\frac{1}{2}$ × 70$\frac{7}{8}$".
Musée d'Art Moderne de la Ville de Paris

[3] Aeschylus, "Prometheus Unbound" in *Greek Plays in Modern Translation*, ed. by Dudley Fitts, trans. by Edith Hamilton, Dial, New York, 1947, pp. 538–39.

There is no "message" in Tamayo's work beyond that. It is poignant, pervasive, and sufficient. But he states it with a strange mixture of the subjective and the objective. Here again we come to a paradox. His forms are violent, punctuated by bold, repetitive linear passages, but his colors are jewel-rich, and the textural nuances of his often thin pigments are of extraordinary sensibility and sensuality. Yet this sensuality is not a superficial softening agent. The colors and textures make for a shimmering, transfiguring luminosity. The linear patterns seem to be antennae, reaching to catch every vibration in the atmosphere. The astonishing thing is that Tamayo's "message" is not diluted by his pictures' physical opulence but reinforced by it. The immediate impact of his pictures is, in truth, of an elegance comparable to that in a still life by Georges Braque. Only on longer viewing does the spectator become aware that the quivering figures, spare and feverish enough to suggest burning wax candles, are not just stylized abstracted shapes in a composition, that their setting is something more than a flickering surface mysteriously charged with energy, and that they have meaning beyond their substance as formal compositions of striking power and richness.

It is also impossible, on restudying many paintings by Tamayo whose shapes did not clearly identify themselves when they were first done, to avoid recognizing and reading them years later as uncannily clairvoyant projections of events that were not actually to happen for a long time. In 1954, for example, he painted a picture he called *The Astronomer* (plate 6). It is an uncharacteristically dark, brooding, mysterious canvas, mostly in rust browns, with arclike streaks of gray and brief touches of blood red. Except for a small shape at the left, recalling Auguste Piccard's stratospheric balloon, its surface is largely given to a whirling, fearsome, sharply faceted geometric form, somewhat suggesting the head of a man but also carrying a clearly animal-like image spiraling through space. Three years *after* it was painted the Russians launched their Sputnik satellite containing a dog whose physical reactions to weightlessness could be recorded by Soviet scientists. Invariably viewers coming upon Tamayo's *The Astronomer* in exhibitions are astonished at what they first see as an atypically "realistic" (for him), if complex, painting of Sputnik carrying the dog Laika, of man himself in

lunar orbit, and of two spacecraft in a docking action. Tamayo smiles, shrugs his shoulders. Far too modest to call himself a visionary, he is hardly of the breed of documentary space painters whom the National Aeronautics and Space Administration had been inviting to its headquarters at Houston and to the launching pad at Cape Canaveral to record their observations and impressions of lunar flight.

It is, incidentally, an interesting fact that Tamayo *was* one of a very special group of six artists of international repute who were also invited to make a special trip to NASA headquarters, not to record their observations in paintings or drawings but rather to meet with scientists and discuss the relationship between science and art on a theoretical level. Marcel Duchamp, curiously, was among them, and, although it was imaginative of the conference planners to ask the father of Dada to be part of it, one wonders what contribution was expected of a professed anti-artist. For the half century since he painted his famous *Nude Descending a Staircase* and shortly thereafter turned away from art altogether, Duchamp had spent his time playing chess. In any case, the other artists present, in deference to Duchamp's age and his almost mythical place in the history of modern art, let him speak for them. As Tamayo recalls the event, Duchamp's position was that artists don't know what they do, or why, or whether it is any good. "It is the people who tell us what we are doing," he said. Tamayo protested this reply. His own conviction is that almost every artist of worth knows precisely what he is doing, as did Duchamp, perhaps more than most, since his work is entirely intellectual, revealing nothing of heart or fantasy. Even his "caprice," as Tamayo calls it, was always deliberate.

It is not farfetched to wonder whether Tamayo's almost total absorption with forms in space, his recurring images of man facing the firmament, may spring from something within him even deeper and older than his obsession with a world being choked to death by technology and its ecological, holocaustic wake. Could it not have its subconscious origin in his passion for Mexico's Pre-Columbian art and architecture? Temples, ancient stones, and codices tell us of the Mexican Indians' phenomenal knowledge of astronomy and of the accuracy of their calculations about planetary paths. Their computations on the

movement of Venus in relation to the earth are said to have been so precise that modern scientists find a margin of error of just a single day in their projections for six thousand years. Their religion, their agriculture, the whole social fabric of their daily lives were completely bound up with astronomical calculations and forecasts and with the mystery and the power of the sun and the moon.

Once more, then, we have an instance of the duality of Tamayo's nature. He is, very likely, the only artist of international stature who is completely the product of the twentieth-century aesthetic revolution and yet, at the same time, draws his strength and substance from a primitive tradition that is entirely his own. Picasso, Braque, Gris, and others among the younger, revolutionary painters in Paris about 1906 and 1907, had taken provocative departures in form and expressiveness suggested to them by the African primitive art they found on exhibition in ethnographic collections. Largely out of these discoveries Cubism was formulated. Primitive arts of all sorts have never lost their enormous impact as source and inspiration for twentieth-century artists. But the response was intellectual and formal. The artists knew very little, if anything, about the informing beliefs and rituals behind the works which spurred their own highly productive experiments.

Tamayo's involvement in the ancient art of Mexico had started when he was twenty-one, and he left the San Carlos Academy of Fine Arts, in Mexico City, because he found its teaching program too academic. Soon after this he was appointed head of the department of ethnographical drawing of the National Museum of Archaeology. He recalls these days warmly.

> We had a great man at that time—José Vasconcelos, who was appointed Minister of Education by Mexico's new president, Obregón. He established our open-air rural school system, and he inaugurated the mural program. He didn't necessarily believe in the great genius of the men who were commissioned to paint Mexico's walls, but he gave them the opportunity, and for two reasons. He wanted to help develop art and artists in Mexico, drawing on Mexico's own heritage

6. *The Astronomer*. 1954. 23½ × 29½″. Collection Mr. and Mrs. Frederick Gash, New York

instead of on themes and techniques borrowed but not assimilated from foreign cultures. He also felt that people needed the propaganda message that would be contained in the murals. He and I came from the same town, Oaxaca, and he liked me. It was he who gave me, when I was twenty-one, the first job I ever had, working in the archaeological museum. At that time I was still a student at the Academy.

At the museum I was really put into immediate and daily contact with the Pre-Columbian art which before then, of course, I had seen—you can't miss it in either Oaxaca or Mexico City or anyplace else in Mexico—but which I had never truly related to or understood. But even before that I had realized at the Academy that my training wasn't doing me any good. It was thoroughly European. The school's director had lived abroad for some time and worked in the manner of the Barbizon painters and the Impressionists. The classes at the Academy still used a method of instruction known as the Pillet system, which meant that students were trained to comprehend some abstract notion of the beauties of line, form, and color, separated from natural forms. It sounds as if it might have been a good system, leading to the really sound principles of abstract composition, but actually it was a dry, academic, lifeless system that had been developed for use in elementary schools in France.

Then I went to the museum, where my little office was in the middle of the great Pre-Columbian collections. There I was surrounded by objects that were a revelation to me. They made me realize that everything I had been taught in school was useless, at least for me. The technical facility was useless. I had to forget all I had been taught and learn to do things in a new way, a more difficult way, so I wouldn't be trapped by facility. I absorbed the new influence, almost subconsciously, in emotional, spiritual, intellectual, and technical ways simultaneously.

I realized that there was a great beauty in those objects, and it had nothing to do with what we had been taught in

school—things like classical proportions, for example, where the head is one-seventh of the whole body. I saw that the rule of one-seventh works for classical art, but that in other kinds of art the proportions are different. In South Seas art the formula works in just the opposite way. The head is six-sevenths, and the body is one-seventh. The mystical seven remains, but with the small proportion playing against the whole. There were no other artists in Mexico at that time who were thinking along these lines or felt its mystery. In 1921 I was the only one.

Tamayo's job at the museum, despite his title as head of the department of ethnographical drawing, had specifically to do with preserving the purity of design of Mexican folk arts and crafts. Tourists were beginning to visit Mexico in great numbers at that time, and they bought many Mexican objects. Tamayo was assigned to set up small museums of old art objects in towns and villages about the country, so that craftsmen working at pottery, textiles, and other crafts could follow the ancient designs and retain ancient traditions.

Along with the new approach to form that he derived from continued and intense involvement with the old arts was an empathy with the deeply human elements of Pre-Columbian art—the experiences, practices, social system, superstitions, fears, myths, and beliefs of the varied peoples who had made the great arts of Mexico before the Spanish Conquest. All these, Tamayo feels, and not the Zapotecs alone, were his ancestors. And so, as has already been pointed out, presently it became impossible for him to continue in the conventional ways he had been taught and was already finding fruitless. By 1931 he began to paint heavy, hieratically still figures clearly related in their form to Pre-Columbian sculpture and pottery and in their color to what he insists is the real palette of Mexico, muted and austere, as opposed to the bright colors generally associated with the country (plate 7).

Mexicans are not gay, as people think we are. That gaiety is reserved only for our fiestas. In essence we are a very tragic people, who have been subdued again and again by outside

forces. If it was not the Spanish, it was the French, or the Americans. We were always oppressed, and our sadness, which you can see in the Indians particularly, is expressed in our colors.

But these colors also have to do with economics. Travelers in small villages throughout Mexico must see that the houses are painted in a limited palette—whites, blues, sometimes ocher yellow, maybe even pink. The reason is that these are very cheap colors, the only ones the people can afford. The materials are very cheap, too. The women's rebozos are generally blue, or gray, or black. Notice any crowd of Mexicans, especially in a small village, and you will see that blue, white, and a little pink predominate. Only at fiesta time can the people afford to break out into brighter colors. If I wanted my art to be universal but still to speak with Mexican accents, it had to draw on more than the facts of history or sociology or journalism. It had to grow out of everything that was truly Mexican. It had to grow out of something in my own blood, in my sensibility and vision, fed from my childhood by objects not quite seen or felt, as well as by my consciousness of them later on, when I became truly aware of their meaning and kept seeing them at every turn of my head.

Tamayo was born and spent his childhood in Oaxaca, a city in the southwestern province of Mexico also called Oaxaca. Geographically situated between the terrain of the Mayans in the south and that of the Aztecs to the north, the fertile, semitropical Valley of Oaxaca was inhabited as early as A.D. 250 by Zapotecs and by Mixtecs. Very close to the city, on a magnificent ceremonial acropolis overlooking the valley, is the site of ancient Monte Alban, one of the greatest concentrations of monumental tombs and temples in all Mexico. Mitla, another majestic ancient site associated with the Mixtecs, is also nearby. (It is because of his great love of his picturesque native city in southern Mexico, and because its nearness to Monte Alban and Mitla has made Oaxaca both a source of immense pride to its inhabitants and a strong magnet for tourists, that Tamayo in 1974 presented the city with a splendid

7. *Woman in Grey.* 1931. $86\frac{1}{2} \times 64''$.
    Collection the artist

8. *Woman*. Pre-Columbian, from Southern Nayarit. Burnished clay with traces of black paint, height, 19″. Collection Stendahl, Los Angeles

museum of pre-Spanish art. It is located in a handsome late sixteenth-century Colonial mansion he bought and superbly restored. In its handsome galleries are two thousand examples of pre-Spanish ceramics and sculpture made in all the areas of Mexico before the conquest. These, too, which Tamayo has been collecting for twenty years, he gave as a gift to the people of Oaxaca. It is a museum unique in Mexico in that it displays Pre-Columbian art in a primarily aesthetic context, instead of stressing its archaeological and ethnographic aspects.)

Tamayo was only twelve years old, however, when his parents died and he went to Mexico City to live with an unmarried aunt who ran a shop in the marketplace, where she sold tropical fruits from the south and where he helped her after school hours. It was a hard life, and the boy found release and joy singing in the church, drawing, and playing the guitar, which he taught himself. At his primary school, art classes were taught, but the teachers were not artists, and the training was in no way professional. Most of the time he copied postcards, doing it, he recalls, in the most difficult way, using hard, sharp pencils, simply because he knew no better. Learning the guitar was no easier. He knew nothing about fingering and had to discover chords by himself, but he became a good guitarist and on occasion still plays for his friends. When he was fifteen, his aunt sent him to commercial school, thinking that he would eventually assist her in running her shop. Instead, he secretly attended classes at the San Carlos Academy of Fine Arts, where, as he has told us, teaching methods were hardly better than they had been in the art classes of his primary school.

When he was twenty-one, he realized that he was almost at a dead end in Mexico City. The Academy, where the first year was given to painting what were called, as he translates the Spanish phrase used, "usual objects" and the second to "coloring," offered nothing to a boy already certain that art would be his lifework, that he had something to say, and that he had to find a way to say it.

There was the example of the older men to inspire him. Rivera had returned to Mexico from his stay and studies in Paris in 1920. While abroad, he had worked in the Cubist style, although his Cubist pictures were not being exhibited in Mexico. To Tamayo, Rivera's example

34

9. *Chair with Fruit.* 1929.
$28\frac{1}{2} \times 25''$.
Collection the artist

served primarily as reassurance that it was possible to break with the past. On his return to Mexico, Rivera saw Tamayo's work in a student exhibition at the Academy and made a point of informing the instructors that this was the one student to be encouraged and watched. Rivera also served briefly as director of the Academy, attempting unsuccessfully to revise and renew the teaching system.

There was at this time no contact in Mexico City with what young artists in Paris were doing. Communications were virtually non-existent. Tamayo had heard that Picasso, Braque, and other artists of the School of Paris were interested in primitive arts, but none of their work was to be seen in Mexico City at this time aside from a few poor reproductions which occasionally turned up. Tamayo himself was involved in what he refers to now as "so-called Mexican characteristics." It was not until 1926, when he arrived in New York for the first time, that he saw originals of the new painting in Paris.

Before that, however, he had become an art teacher in Mexico City. His own works were chiefly the weighty, inert figure pieces he had been moved to paint through his contact with primitive sculptures (plate 8) and brightly colored fruit still lifes reflecting the long hours he had spent helping his aunt in her tropical fruit shop (plate 9). His themes were static, but his compositions grew steadily more animated as he began to play shapes and echoing lines against one another to create a back-and-forth compositional movement even in pictures that had no depicted action but only the plastic activity he himself set in motion.

In 1926 he had his first exhibition. It was in an empty shop in Mexico City, since there were no art galleries there at that time. Later that same year he determined that he must go to New York. He made the journey with his friend Carlos Chávez, later, of course, a celebrated composer and eventually Minister of Fine Arts in the government, but at the time a young, struggling pianist. Together they decided to remain in New York, taking a loft in a shabby Fourteenth Street tenement where other painters lived. Marcel Duchamp, Stuart Davis, Reginald Marsh, and Yasuo Kuniyoshi were close neighbors, and Tamayo came to know all of them well.

It was through his conversations with them and his first real

exposure to the kind of art he had known so far only through faulty reproductions, that Tamayo began to think of his art as being a Mexican expression which might also be international. "The world opened up to me in New York," he says. The result would be incalculably important to his development. It would lead in time to a revision of his style to the point where, while retaining his national and racial traditions in the formal terms of color and shape, his preoccupation would be less consciously with Mexican roots and origins than with the whole contemporary world. Later on, his colors began to change too, growing brighter and more resonant—more "shocking" is his own word for the change—and eventually, in line with his more universal outlook, his shapes changed too, growing less literal and weighty and more transparent and insubstantial.

All that, however, was to come much later. In the beginning the problem in New York was just to live. Although Chávez was able to get a job playing the organ in a motion-picture house, the two had an extremely difficult time financially. Chávez, a fine pianist but poor organist, Tamayo says, was not equipped to do the kind of thing required of him, and when he turned his hand to popular music to make some money, publishers were not at all receptive. Nevertheless, Chávez did come to know important figures in the world of music, among them the composer Edgard Varèse, whose portrait Tamayo painted. And Tamayo looked up the artist and critic Walter Pach, whom he had met when Pach spent some time in Mexico working on a book. It was Pach who took Tamayo with him to the Weyhe Book Shop on upper Lexington Avenue, which also operates on its premises a small but fine art gallery, and which, one month after his arrival in New York, offered to give the astonished young painter a one-man exhibition.

Modest as it was, Weyhe's at that time had—even as it still does—an excellent reputation, and exhibition there carried sufficient prestige to draw the city's art critics. They received Tamayo's show of small watercolors favorably, but there were no sales. Carl Zigrosser, director of the gallery, then suggested to Tamayo that he do some woodcuts, and these, in fact, sold well.

Launched now on a New York career, Tamayo remained in the

city for two years. His closest associates there were two friends from Mexico, Chávez and the caricaturist Miguel Covarrubias. He also began to meet more Americans, among them an art dealer, Mrs. Frances Paine, who had been instrumental in setting up something called the Mexican Arts Association, designed to maintain a permanent exhibition of Mexican fine and applied arts in New York. Through her excellent social and financial connections Mrs. Paine was able to get Tamayo a commission to design fabrics for a large manufacturer, and, more interesting, to design a Mexican ballet with music by Chávez. The ballet never materialized, although Tamayo received a five-hundred-dollar fee anyway. Suddenly he found himself with some money and recognition, and, most important, in a sympathetic, responsive environment where he felt enormously alive.

In 1928 he became ill and returned to Mexico. On recovering, he took a teaching post at the National School of Fine Arts there, where Rivera was now serving as director. Together they worked to improve teaching methods until in 1930 both artists left the Academy. Tamayo, whose interest in teaching art was now serious, two years later became chief of the government's department of plastic arts, where he would institute new methods of teaching art to children.

Something curious happened to his art after his return to Mexico. Away from the influence of New York's cosmopolitan art world, his painting became more "Mexican" again. He grew interested, for one thing, in Mexican popular arts (as distinct from the traditional folk arts that had occupied him earlier). Themes out of everyday urban life attracted him, even something as banal as the painted backgrounds used in Mexico City photographers' studios, an interest that continued for several years (plate 10).

By 1930 he was back in New York, remaining there long enough to have a second exhibition, this time at the John Levy Gallery. In 1933, once more in Mexico, he was commissioned to paint a mural for the National School of Music. While working on that commission, he met a young piano student, whom he married early the following year. In 1934, Olga and Rufino Tamayo went up to New York together, with the idea that he would paint and she would continue her music studies.

38

10. *Nina Bonita.* 1937.
$53\frac{1}{8} \times 37\frac{3}{8}''$.
Collection Maria Rogers, New York

11. *Meeting*. 1960. $38\frac{1}{8} \times 51\frac{1}{8}''$. Collection the artist

But by this time the United States had plunged deeply into a bitter economic depression. Living in New York had become extremely difficult. The young couple spent their first week in New York occupying a grimy, rag-hung room on West Eighth Street in Greenwich Village over a restaurant that was known as Romany Marie's. Even in the middle thirties it still served as a meeting place for artists and intellectuals, as it had been when it was the haunt of Eugene O'Neill, among others, many years earlier.

From there the couple moved to quarters on Fourteenth Street, only a little more attractive, although they remained there for a year. Their rent, Olga Tamayo still remembers, was fifty dollars a month, and they were able to hold their expenses down to another fifty dollars. Tamayo had by this time found employment on the Federal Arts Project of the Works Progress Administration, established by the United States government as an emergency economic measure to provide regular incomes to needy artists in return for a specified number of works which would belong to the government. A great many American artists of first-class reputation at that time, and many younger ones who were given the opportunity for gaining a foothold and growing when otherwise this might have been impossible, were employed on what they still refer to with nostalgia and gratitude as "The Project." Tamayo, like the others, received a monthly stipend of about a hundred dollars, on which he and his bride managed to live. He was obligated to give the government only a single watercolor a month. In view of the prices his works would eventually command, the generous arrangement that made productive life possible for him in New York proved to be a very good deal for the government, too. (This was true also of scores of other artists employed on the project.)

Before long, however, Tamayo was fired on the principle that, as a foreigner, he was not entitled to assistance. Again he was forced to return to Mexico. Then once more, in 1936, this time with Siqueiros and Orozco, he came back, to serve as a delegate representing the Mexican League of Revolutionary Painters and Artists at an American Artists' Congress held in New York.

It was about then, Tamayo recalls, that he first felt impelled to

12. *The Sky.* 1960.
$53\frac{1}{8} \times 76\frac{3}{4}''$.
Private collection, Paris

paint pictures having to do not with pictorial space but with actual space. He is not certain why, although his memory is that his interest might have been stirred in the early thirties by the highly publicized transoceanic flights of the dirigibles *Graf Zeppelin* and *Hindenburg*.

By now he had many friends in New York. The Julien Levy Gallery offered him an exhibition in 1937, to follow immediately after its first and historic showing of Salvador Dali's work. Other exhibitions took place, in San Francisco and Chicago. Back briefly in Mexico City, Tamayo was commissioned to paint a mural for the archaeological museum, although it was never actually executed.

By 1936 what had become virtually a life of commuting changed. In 1938 Carlos Dávila, a friend who had formerly been president of Chile and now lived in New York, proposed him for a teaching job at the highly esteemed and progressive Dalton School, where Dávila was a member of the board of trustees and his two small daughters were students. It was an ideal situation for Tamayo, since his teaching hours ran from eight in the morning until noon, and thereafter he was free to paint.

But the pictures piled up in the corner of his studio unsold. Valentine Dudensing, whose gallery was at that time one of New York's most

42

13.   *The Offering.* 1969. $31\frac{1}{2} \times 39\frac{3}{8}''$. Perls Galleries, New York

prestigious, in 1939 invited Tamayo to exhibit there. He did, but while showing at the Valentine, as the gallery was called, was a very considerable distinction for the young artist, the exhibition again brought no sales. Nevertheless, the Dalton School teaching post, where he remained for nine years, made life in New York not only possible and productive but also agreeable. The Tamayos moved to an apartment on the upper East Side. They entertained frequently and hospitably at parties, where Tamayo played his guitar and Olga served Mexican food she prepared herself. Soon their friends began to include not only painters but collectors as well. Among them was Samuel A. Lewisohn, at that time a vice-president and trustee of the Museum of Modern Art, who added pictures by Tamayo to his celebrated collection of Post-Impressionist and twentieth-century works. Other sales to well-known collectors followed. Members of the Rockefeller family bought pictures they would eventually present to the Museum of Modern Art. Lee Ault and Ralph Colin added Tamayo canvases to their collections. New York's important Whitney Museum of American Art invited Tamayo to participate in its annual survey of paintings by Americans, although he himself, despite his long years of residence here, never thought of himself as anything but Mexican.

It was in the early forties that Tamayo, painting the human figure, began breaking it up into fragments. It was not a departure with thematic significance. He was not yet thinking of human beings as bodies emotionally torn apart by their own or the world's problems. He was totally involved with shapes and their accommodation into composition. And the shapes, patterns, and relationships between them which he evolved would recur in his art for the next thirty years, appearing even in his most recent canvases, so unlike his early work. One of many instances is his use of areas of dark parallel lines, horizontally, like rungs in a ladder, or vertically, like the flutings in a Classical column. In the early work they may be precisely that—rungs in a ladder, or the posts of a balcony (plate 10), or the strings of a guitar. In later paintings it would be difficult to give them specific identity; now they are simply design elements that may set space vibrating, break up color passages, establish visual direction lines, hold compositions together (plate 11). In his early works Tamayo

frequently introduced fruits, such as a cut watermelon, into his still lifes because his composition might need a red area to combine with other reds. With the passing of years he became free enough to discard "logical" or representational justifications. Now he introduces a spot of red simply because his picture needs it. At one point, late in the forties, Tamayo felt that he had become so overly concerned with design requirements that he often thereafter all but discarded linear and color patterns altogether, dissolving contours in an allover vaporous haze. He has continued to move back and forth from one "mood" to another, concentrating now on texture (plate 12), another time on line, and then moving in some other direction until he feels he has found a proper balance. In the same way, even in recent years, he may paint a fairly literal theme, as in the study of what he describes as a man opening his heart (plate 13) and in another of a figure coiled in telephone wires, sick of the disease of our time that Tamayo calls "telephonitis" (plate 14). But then he slips out of his literalism to paint an image that defies identification altogether except in the broadest terms, as the personification of agony, or violence, or flight, or just the wind.

Early on, however, Tamayo's involvement in stern, self-imposed problems of theme and design was heightened by a series of major mural commissions. His themes for these were never narrowly didactic, historical, or rhetorical, as in the paintings of Rivera, Siqueiros, and most of the other muralists in Mexico. Tamayo's murals were symbolic, treating "big truths" such as man, art, nature. All three of these are combined in one mural in 1943 for Smith College, Northampton, Massachusetts, the first of many murals he would execute in the United States (plate 15). Filling a large end of the Hillyer Art Library, the surface of this mural was chiefly given to a large, reclining, four-breasted nude female figure representing Nature and meant to symbolize abundance. Surrounding her are four highly stylized minor figures personifying Water (the blue figure at the left holding a stream), Lightning (the red figure above her), Earth (the tan half-figure behind her supporting the major figure), and Air (the blue figure at the right, slender and straight as an arrow). Curving over the whole composition is a rainbow to symbolize color, which is, as Tamayo himself defines it, "the basic element of painting." At the

14. *Telephonitis* (*The Operator*).
1957. $39\frac{3}{8} \times 31\frac{1}{2}''$.
Nasjonalgalleriet, Oslo,
Norway

extreme right of the reclining nude is a male half-figure, representing the artist at work on a picture. Between the artist and Nature may be seen the shapes of a lyre, for music, and a compass, for science. Tamayo saw them, he explained, as denoting imagination and knowledge. The extreme right end of the panel depicts another figure, symbolizing a work of art, its diagonal body sharply inclined toward the rest of the composition. Between this figure and the artist at his easel is "the observer," his eyes, according to a letter written by Tamayo at the time, "fixed on the work itself, to the complete exclusion of his surroundings. This is to emphasize the idea that when judging a work of art one must take it as a new creation, independent of the source from which it sprang. The observer stands with his back to the group that symbolizes Nature."

The Smith College mural was worked out so schematically, conforming so strictly to the old principle of the "golden section" as to remind us of Tamayo's feeling of revelation years before, when he discovered that the ancient formula for proportion he had learned from Greek casts applied, with a reversal of factors, to primitive art as well. It also establishes how early he employed highly stylized, almost abstract form to project concrete idea. It suggests, too, that the theme for the mural was an intellectual rather than emotional concept springing from his spirit. The resulting composition was extremely strong, perhaps even overwhelming for its setting and its space.

In 1946 Tamayo began to teach at the Brooklyn Museum Art School, and a new pattern of living took shape. Winters were spent in New York, summers in Mexico, with time out for travel and for attending the exhibitions of his work beginning to be held frequently in other cities in America as well as abroad. In 1949 he went to Europe for the first time. The year before that the Valentine Gallery had ceased operating, and Tamayo was invited to exhibit at the Pierre Matisse Gallery, owned in New York by the son of Henri Matisse. In 1950 Tamayo had the signal honor of having a gallery devoted solely to his work at that year's Biennale in Venice, the most important series of international art exhibitions in the world. By then he was internationally established as a major artist.

For some five years before this Tamayo had been working toward a much more dynamic approach to composition than had marked his pictures earlier. His figures, more fragmented than ever, began to take on a new buoyancy, as if they were frantically leaping, bounding, flying through space, reaching out wildly to grasp, hold, encompass the whole terrifying cosmos (plates 16, 17, 18, 19). The introduction of stylized birds heightened the connotation of space, as did clusters and networks of constellations. The moon became almost a fixed feature of his composition, giving off an eerie light as if from it stemmed all madness. Eventually the moon would disappear from his pictures as a visible source of light, although its infernal luminosity would remain.

By that time the Tamayo story had become one of more and more exhibitions (in Mexico City, in New York, in South America, and in Europe, where, in 1968, he was honor guest at the Venice Biennale and accorded an exhibition of 70 paintings); of more and more prizes (including a shared grand prize in 1953 at the São Paulo Bienal; second prize in 1955 at the Carnegie International Exhibition in Pittsburgh; the Guggenheim International Foundation Prize and International Prize at the Mexico City Biennial, both in 1960; and the Mexican government's Premio Nacional in 1964); and many more mural commissions. In 1952 he was asked to paint a mural for Mexico City's Palace of Fine Arts, which already contained murals by Rivera, Orozco, and Siqueiros. The following year he was asked to contribute a second one for the same building. The first of them, titled *The Birth of Nationality* (plate 20), symbolically treats the birth of Mexican nationality out of Spanish and Indian seeds, and the second is called *Mexico Today* (plate 21). They were, when first painted, and remain even today, an extraordinary addition to the works in the same spacious hall by Rivera, Orozco, and Siqueiros, all countless yards of Spanish conquistadores, capitalist exploiters, downtrodden workers and peasants, the dead, the maimed, and the chained. Tamayo's own conceptions are so highly stylized as to seem, at first viewing, almost abstract compositions of glowing color rising from deep, resonant purples at the base to almost phosphorescent greens at the top. Next one feels the flowing, swinging, rhythmic movement of the forms. In *The Birth of Nationality* one then perceives these as a white figure on

48

horseback extending almost across the entire canvas in a composition including various architectural fragments; a fetus-like shape, half white and half brown; and, above all, a double sun. The horse and rider represent the Spanish invaders who came to the new land on horseback, causing the Indians, who had never seen horses before, to regard them as strange, supernatural, centaur-like creatures. In *Mexico Today* the shapes carry the same theme further, symbolizing the Indian and Spanish contributions to art, building, agriculture, and science in contemporary Mexico.

Tamayo had a formidable physical job in composing the murals. Not only is the Palace of Fine Arts a structure of monstrous ugliness, but also, standing squarely in front of the spaces allotted to his murals were obtrusive beige marble columns that could not be removed. Therefore he had to conceive his compositions so that, when viewed close up, they appear totally integrated, and yet, viewed from a distance through the obstructive columns, they suggest panel pictures separated by the columns. He had come a long way from the Smith College mural, in which he had not yet learned to accept and work within existing architectural elements.

There was an important by-product from these two mural commissions. The preceding year Tamayo had been asked by the Mexican government's National Institute of Fine Arts, a body corresponding to a fine-arts ministry, to contribute paintings to a major survey of Mexican art planned for presentation in Paris. Intransigent in his belief that his government's art-patronage program had become unprogressive and shortsighted, he replied that before consenting to take part he would like to know whether the Paris exhibition was to be an "official" government project and, if so, what the government's official art position was.

As Tamayo himself tells the story, a lengthy silence followed, punctuated by his repeated requests for clarification, and ended at last by a letter from Fernando Gamboa, assistant general director of the National Institute, stating that this was, indeed, to be an official showing, that the position of the government was to support all art of quality and not just polemical art, and that as evidence of its sincerity, the government was inviting Tamayo to paint the two large murals in the Palace

15. *Nature and the Artist.*
1943. Mural.
Smith College Museum of Art,
Northampton, Mass.

16. *Cataclysm.*
1946. $24\frac{1}{8} \times 20''$.
Collection Pablo Brener,
Mexico City

of Fine Arts. Tamayo did, then, contribute his pictures to the Paris exhibition, where they were received with immense enthusiasm. Immediately thereafter he started work on the Mexico City panels. They represent, he felt at the time, a battle won not for himself but for the cause of art and Mexico.

Other mural commissions followed in quick succession, Tamayo embracing the opportunity to paint heroic themes on a heroic scale. Their treatment was never either literal or rhetorical. Always their first and most commanding aspect was of sensuous color and vibrant coherent forms. In 1953 he painted an impressive panel called *Man* for the Dallas Museum of Fine Arts in Texas (plate 45).

Two years later he executed an even larger work (64 by 14 feet) called *America* for the Bank of the Southwest in Houston, Texas (plate 22). He describes its theme as America, represented by a figure in its lower section, surrounded by the sea. "Because of its great proportions," he says, "this figure conveys the ideal of abundance, the main characteristic of our continent. Abundance is shown too by the fish, symbol of the wealth of the sea; by a plant, symbol of the richness of our land; by an oil geyser and a spring of water, symbols of our underground resources. In the upper part of the mural two embracing figures signify the melting of America's two basic races, whose cultural contributions enrich her spiritually. The figure at the left, in white, is the white race, and next to it is the cross, symbol of Occidental culture. The figure at the right, in brown, is the Indian race, whose contribution is represented by the plumed serpent Quetzalcoatl, symbol of Pre-Columbian culture."

A mural on the theme of Prometheus was painted on canvas in 1957 for installation in the library of the University of Puerto Rico. The following year Tamayo completed a large mural for the UNESCO headquarters building in Paris. Among the most distinguished and most important of several others he has executed since then are one called *Duality* (plates 23, 24), for the magnificent new National Museum of Anthropology in Mexico City, a panel for the Mexican pavilion at Montreal's Expo '67, and murals for the Industrial Club of Mexico, the last being perhaps the most abstract he has ever done, an expanse of enormously animated flamelike forms expressing industrial energy

17. *Woman in the Night.*
1947. 39 × 28″.
Collection Pablo Brener,
Mexico City

(plate 25). His most recent mural, entitled *Man Confronting Infinity* (plate 26), is for the new Camino Real Hotel in Mexico City.

Over the years there was a continuing flow of easel pictures, in that extraordinary outpouring of energy which occasionally marks the works of great artists as they grow older. There were many voyages, years of residence in Paris, and, eventually, a return to Mexico to make his permanent home.

From this point on—or even earlier—external events were, to Tamayo's mind, of no great consequence. The things seen had either been absorbed to the degree that they might affect his own expression, or rejected. His gifts had been acclaimed about the world. His home was established and his working patterns were set. These are, he says, those of a craftsman, with no waiting for inspiration, since technique itself has always to be exercised and improved. Eight hours each day, therefore, he spends in the studio which is part of his home, beginning directly after an early breakfast, pausing briefly for lunch, and returning to the studio to work until late afternoon. The only interruptions he permits are from a few dealers, artists, and others he knows who bring him finds of Pre-Columbian art of sufficient quality to interest him and, they hope, tempt him into adding them to his already enormous collections.

The vital things that would happen to Tamayo from then on would happen in his mind as he studied his own efforts, as he thought about events in the outside world, and as he let the interplay of the two work on his consciousness and emotions. To a surprising degree those events in the outside world, stunning in their impact, seemed of a piece with his preoccupations for several years preceding them. The invention of the sonic aircraft, for instance, with its concomitant images of man maddened and shattered by its vibrations, seemed almost a confirmation of Tamayo's prophetic vision of trembling man in space.

As he reflected on both his art and the world, he was also confirmed in his conviction that an artist must be concerned with communication, and that this must be done through the emotions of his viewers rather than through their minds alone. If an artist has something that is important for him to say, and he says it powerfully and well, the public

18.   *Women Reaching for the Moon.*
1946. $36\frac{1}{4} \times 26''$.
The Cleveland Museum of Art.
Gift of Hanna Fund, 1947

19. *Dancer in the Night.*
1950. 70 × 50″.
Museum of Modern Art,
Caracas, Venezuela

will receive this and respond, even if unprepared by critical exegesis and in a way it can never respond to the factual presentations of history or journalism.

I believe this applies even to the murals put up by our government expressly to stir the people. They didn't do that, although they may have informed the public. But I'm not certain even of that. The people of Mexico who have occasion to go to our public buildings at all (mostly they're officials who have business with the government) hurry in and out of them, with no time or inclination to look at the paintings on the walls. Certainly the peasants don't see them. And yet you have only to watch these same people at the Archaeological Museum in Mexico City to see how deeply they can respond to art. I must add here, perhaps immodestly, that I have observed them studying my own mural at the museum, and many of them coming to my exhibitions, too, and I notice that they respond to color and forms and the overall mood, even if my themes may not be immediately clear. The senses of ordinary people may be more educated than we realize, more so, perhaps, than those of many so-called educated people. The average person recognizes and responds to what touches the roots of human experience.

In any case, my themes are usually simple. They deal with man confronted by the mysteries and the terror of the universe. In my earlier work I used to think of man standing in front of his world, still the center of all he saw.

Back in the forties, when I painted the picture of howling, agonized dogs now owned by the Museum of Modern Art, although I took my forms from popular art, I was thinking of mounting world pressures that would soon erupt. I was interested years later that the museum published the picture as one of several by contemporary artists indicating a prescience of the international situation.

Immediately after World War II and the bombings of Hiroshima and Nagasaki, I started thinking about the implications of a new space age and did the first paintings of constellations shooting through space.

Now I think of man confronting not his world but infinity. Perhaps I always did, as many artists in the past did, too. It's just that our idea of infinity has changed. In the religious paintings of the Renaissance infinity was God. Coming down to our own times, infinity seemed for many artists to lie within themselves. The Abstract Expressionists felt that way, I think. But there has to be a point where creator and spectator converge, so they understand each other, and it can't be deep inside the creator's own psyche. In my mind it is this meeting which constitutes "humanism." If "educated" audiences say now that they do understand and respond to Jackson Pollock's inner agonies, I think they may not really be experiencing him but comprehending intellectually what they have been told by critics. Criticism has value, but it's educational. It cannot create or deepen emotional responses, and it should not put into pictures what may not be there. I'm not saying Pollock and the other Abstract Expressionists didn't make a real contribution, because they did. But it was a technical contribution. They explored new ways of handling space and new textural possibilities. Many of their works are also full of energy.

They did something else, too, that was interesting and valid. The United States has little artistic tradition, they said, which is true; therefore let us forget tradition and start from scratch; painting starts with us, now. As a result of their thinking and their work, the United States now occupies a high position in world art which it did not, before. It is particularly Pollock's reexamination of the technical essence of painting that makes him important. Far more so, for instance, than Andrew Wyeth. Wyeth may seem to be a great communicator. But he isn't, at least not on an aesthetic level. He is an illustrator, painting subjects which people remember, or think

they remember. What they respond to in him is a possibility for escape through nostalgia.

I think critics have been responsible for the great importance attached today to such new forms of art as Conceptual, which can actually be interesting. It's not the making of something by hand but its making by man that counts. Most Conceptualists have at least gone into the technological question, which is of huge importance to everybody. But making a little sketch and sending it to a factory or shop for translation into a form is only to fall into the technological trap. It is not the same as shaping a moving, communicable, aesthetic commentary on it. The difference is between a closed and an open experience. A work that has strong impact and nothing more is a closed experience. A work whose impact will stay with the viewer and grow in meaning for him is an open one.

This was just as true of that form of art a few years ago which was the exact opposite of Conceptual art. I mean the art called "accidental." The difference is between form itself—whether it was put together by a machine or by the artist's hand, letting "accidents" happen through dropping or throwing pigment—and form plus content put into that form by a conscious, thinking, and feeling artist who, in fact, let the predetermined form grow out of content, instead of injecting it as an afterthought when the form was finished.

Picasso was great because his art is a total expression of feeling, thinking, heart, soul, brain. And that's why primitive art, for all its tremendous qualities, is not, as a rule, art on the very highest level possible. Its appeal is to the emotions and to the senses but not to the head. And yet, because this appeal is so tremendous, primitive art can, even within its limitations, still be greater than some other expressions which grow only out of the head.

I think of the Purists and of Mondrian, for example. I also think of Pop art, although it's at the other end of the scale. This, too, is a kind of art I respect and find interesting. It is, for

instance, based on something absolutely American, the country's overwhelming concern with business and consumerism. Pop artists found a fountain of inspiration in that, producing a good thing out of a bad thing. But it all started in the mind, and it remains there.

One of the things that does not occupy Tamayo's mind as he thinks about his work in relation to the state of the world and of art is the question of what he calls "newness." Change is not of itself, he feels, a positive value; it must evolve from an artist's work, growing out of where it has been, and from the new experiences he brings to it. Bach and Rembrandt, he points out, "invented" nothing. Rather, they developed what they found into an expression uniquely their own. However, change may have historic importance, and an artist who dares something new is making his own contribution. Tamayo himself sets a much higher value on work that is personal and expressive, even if its development is traditional. The fact is, nevertheless, that he dismisses Rivera, whom he sardonically calls the great "revolutionary," as a painter whose technique was in every brushstroke an extension of Italian Renaissance tradition.

In many senses, of course, Tamayo's own work is traditional, although its heritage (apart, that is, from his strong national roots) would seem to start with Picasso (himself a strong link to the past) and Braque. Picasso he considers by far the greatest artist of our century. As early as 1940 Tamayo's work, possibly as a result of the great Picasso exhibition held that winter at New York's Museum of Modern Art, began, in its boldly rhythmic composition, its angular exaggerations, distortions, and articulations for intensified emotional impact, to suggest that of the Spaniard. Perhaps the importance given to horses and bulls in Picasso's great work *Guernica* (plate 28), painted in 1937 on the theme of the destruction of a defenseless Spanish town by German dive bombers assisting Generalissimo Franco in the Spanish Civil War, was also a contributing factor to Tamayo's increasing use of animals at this time. If so, however, the theme was a reflection filtered through the image, never out of Tamayo's mind's eye, of Pre-Columbian animal sculpture—

the clay dogs from Colima in the western part of the country (plate 27), the Aztec coyotes, the feathered serpents carved in stone everywhere. It is also possible, of course, that Picasso, too, was inspired to a certain extent, perhaps subconsciously, by the treatment of animals in Pre-Columbian art, and that the styles of Picasso and Tamayo very briefly converged in this affinity. In any case, there is a stillness in Tamayo's art at this time, most notably in the figures, that is very unlike Picasso's pictures of the same period. It would be another half-dozen years, about 1946, before Tamayo's figures would lose their rooted look, their air of being immobilized in a role assigned them for eternity, to break out, trembling and quaking, eventually hurling themselves through a terrifyingly hostile milieu, without apparent direction or purpose.

Tamayo, in New York, began about this time to feel more Mexican than he had even in the early days in his own country. His situation was not unique. Marc Chagall has told how he started to feel—and paint, of course—his Russian roots only after he had settled in Paris, his French nationality only after moving to New York during World War II, and his period as a New Yorker only when he had returned permanently to France.

In those years in the thirties and forties when Tamayo felt that his home was in New York in spite of frequent trips back to Mexico, he lived the New York life very intensely. His American friends included Stuart Davis, Ben Shahn, Kuniyoshi, Raphael and Moses Soyer. The European painters who visited in New York, especially the Spanish Surrealist Joan Miró, also became his friends. There are, in fact, suggestions of Miró in some of the works Tamayo painted at this time—works in which stylized and flattened shapes take on a demonic quality and move out into space under a moon in a wide sky. Tamayo holds, however, that Surrealism was not an important influence on him in any way. He saw it as a literal movement, a way of thinking and even of living but not of painting.

Braque, he suggests, may have affected his style more than Miró, although in a general rather than a specific sense. In fact, he regards Braque as the greatest painter of that time because of the way he handled his materials, narrow as that definition of a painter may sound in view

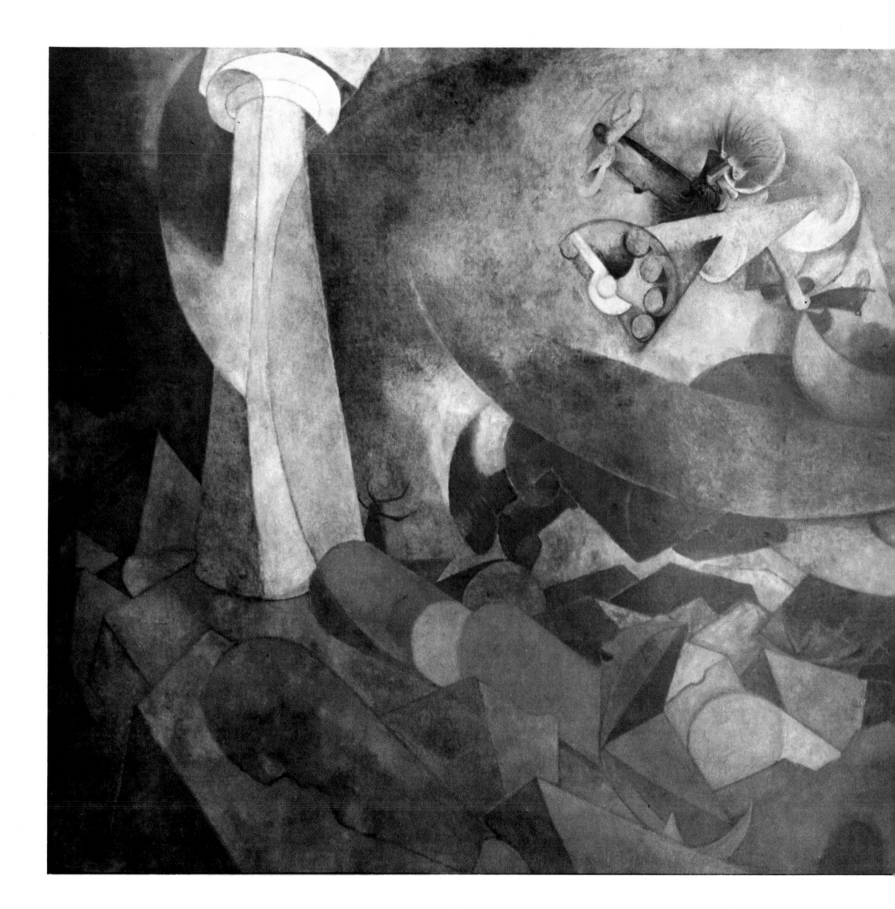

20.   *The Birth of Nationality*. 1952. Mural. Palace of Fine Arts, Mexico City

21. *Mexico Today.* 1953.
Mural. Palace of Fine Arts,
Mexico City

23. *Duality*. 1963–64. Mural. National Museum of Anthropology, Mexico City

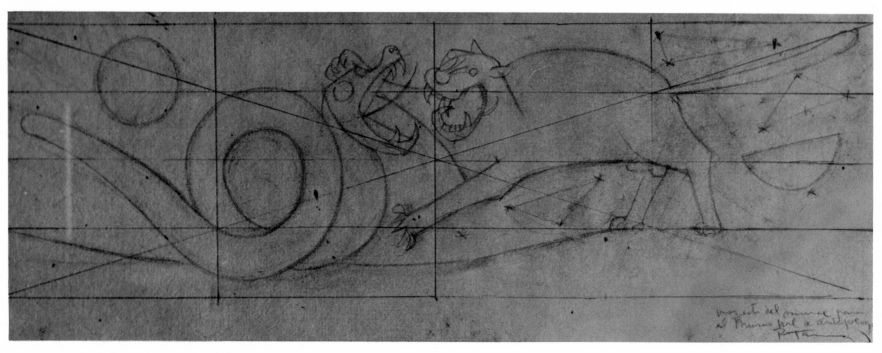

24. Sketch for *Duality*, mural in the National Museum of Anthropology, Mexico City. c. 1964. Pencil on paper, 9½ × 24½″. Bernard Lewin Galleries, Beverly Hills

of Tamayo's own measure of values. Picasso was an inventor, he says, Braque a painter. Limited in his use of materials, which was not surprising in view of his beginnings as apprentice to his father, a painter-decorator, Braque nevertheless extracted from those materials every possibility they held. His ideas and his vision were parochial, as compared with those of Picasso, who explored everywhere, tried everything, and, if unsuccessful, tried again or moved on to something else. Braque knew what he wanted, understood that it was not a big vision, but accomplished his plastic aims brilliantly. Perhaps Tamayo esteems Braque so highly because he has his own big visions, and has found in Braque the rich use of medium that he himself sought early in his career and which still absorbs much of his effort.

Those big visions he treats both as a point of departure and as his destination, never out of his eye for a moment. The course he travels between the two has to do only with painting, not with subject. It has to do with his manipulation of surface, color, texture, in order to make canvases as handsome as he knows how. His theme is so much a part of

25. *Energy.* 1969. Mural. Industrial Club, Mexico City

68

26. *Man Confronting Infinity*. 1971. Mural. Camino Real Hotel, Mexico City

him that he no longer has to think about it consciously. Now he is working with forms, which may grow out of something remembered or felt but must, whatever their source, be adjusted to function within the dimensions of the canvas; with texture, to enrich his surface, if richness is what a particular canvas requires (often, however, his paint is applied very thinly and almost transparently); and with color, which must be developed for its values but always kept flat, so as not to disrupt the two-dimensionality of his picture surfaces. The one thing Tamayo never does with color is to model figures or volumes with it. He may use contour lines for that. More often shapes are determined by the juxtaposition of flat areas of color.

The most difficult technical feat he sets himself is to connote the deep sense of the cosmos which is his recurrent theme, while preserving the flatness of his picture plane. He may do this with rhythmic design sequences such as stabbing diagonals (plate 31), swinging arcs, or labyrinthine linear networks that suggest not only the course of the constellations but also the idea of man caught helpless in a trap (plate 29). He may do it with texture, which may seem to magnify space by suggesting exploding energy (plate 30).

While opening his portrayed space to infinity, he must at the same time firmly establish his composition's cohesiveness. An area of color in one section of a canvas echoed by variations in a carefully measured progression may accomplish this for him. Curling loops of pattern may do it (plate 14), or something as intangible as the vibrations established by all these means working together in a predetermined course but carefully controlled to function within the larger pictorial framework.

Tamayo makes no preliminary drawings for his pictures, working directly on his canvas from the start. But he knows precisely what he wants each picture to look like, and he permits almost no chance developments to govern the results. It is because of his own strong belief in never relaxing control that he considers Picasso "a great artist but a bad painter." Picasso, he says, "would, if he ran out of blue, finish a picture

27. *Dog Scratching Itself.*
Pre-Columbian,
from Colima, Mexico.
Brownish-red clay with traces
of black paint, height, $11\frac{3}{4}''$.
Private collection,
Zurich-Kilchberg, Switzerland

28.   Pablo Picasso. *Guernica.* 1937. Mural. On extended loan to the Museum of Modern Art, New York, from the estate of the artist

29. *Man Looking at the Firmament.*
1957. $39\frac{3}{8} \times 31\frac{1}{2}''$.
Private collection, Rome

30. *Figure.* 1961.
$18\frac{1}{8} \times 21\frac{5}{8}''$.
Collection Bernard Lewin,
Beverly Hills

31. *Night.* 1967.
$37\frac{3}{8} \times 53\frac{1}{8}''$.
Collection Bernard Lewin,
Beverly Hills

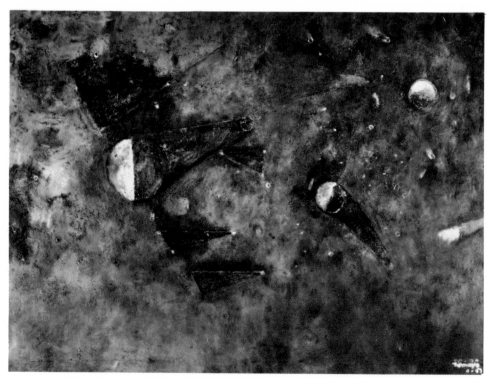

32. *Couple in White.*
1973. 32 × 39$\frac{3}{8}$″.
Perls Galleries, New York

in another color, and it generally worked. I would have decided in advance that blue was precisely what I needed for, say, a certain degree of luminosity. And I would have used blue. It has to do with what I call my own professional approach to painting. I'm not suggesting that I or any other artist should be finicky but that we should be deliberate."

It would never occur to an artist of Tamayo's taste and modesty to equate his painter's approach to a canvas with man's approach to the world we live in. Yet one is struck with the thought that there are parallels, and that a picture itself can, in its very physical existence, be seen as a metaphor of man's refusal to accept a doom that seems increasingly inevitable. The very fact that an artist works, experiments, preserves, is witness to his conviction that the world itself can and must endure, and that if man exercises control over it, it will. If an artist can-

33. *Leader.* 1973. 51 × 38″.
Perls Galleries, New York

not, using mental and manual disciplines, control what happens within the confines of a single one of his works, if he cannot stake out with it one area of order in the midst of chaos, can he dare hope that man will be able to impose some order on his larger environment, on the world itself?

It is hardly likely that Tamayo's ideas of order will change in the work he does in the future. Always he continues to simplify, eliminating from his pictures everything he considers superfluous. Structure, of course, must remain strong. A few years ago he sought structure primarily through texture, but in his most recent canvases there is a new emphasis on incisive line and contour (plates 32, 33).

Another change is apparent in these late pictures. It is a new sense of release, almost of joy (plates 34, 35). Tamayo has come to that stage in his development which so many great painters meet in their advancing age (Cézanne, Picasso, Chagall, Renoir are just a few who come quickly to mind). None of them bound to rules or conventions, once they have found their own idioms, they shake off eventually even their self-imposed

34.   *Three Personages.*
1967. $53\frac{1}{8} \times 76\frac{3}{4}''$.
Private collection

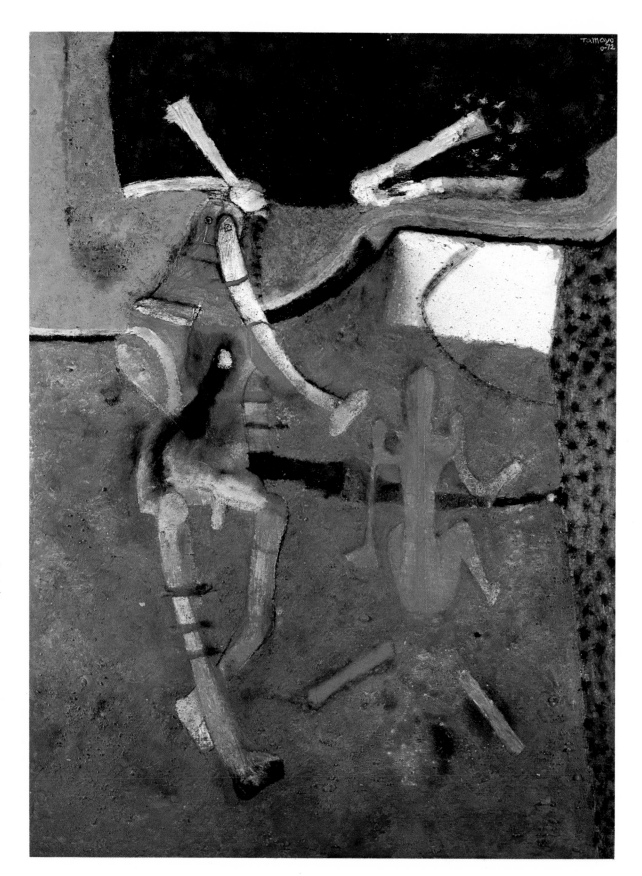

35. *Dancers.* 1972.
$53\frac{1}{8} \times 37\frac{1}{2}''$.
Collection the artist

constraints, not of form but of feeling. A new robustness, spontaneity, and impetuousness enter their work.

In the case of Tamayo the idea of man remains dominant, even if, as in a few pictures of just an exploding sky or eroded earth, man's presence is felt rather than seen. The artist anticipates that man's actual image will almost always remain in his work. The head may be reduced to an oval shape ("a head is plainly a head, even if it doesn't have eyes," Tamayo says); the body may be little more than a vertical band. What he is seeking is that marvelous, mysterious, delicate point at which a human being remains distinctly, recognizably human, relating to other human beings, confronting infinity, but essentially an aggregate of emotions and nerves rather than of distinctive physical characteristics depicted literally.

Tamayo fixes that point in simpler language. "It is the point at which the artist and the spectator meet."

PLATES

36. *Factory*. 1929. 26 × 34″. Collection Pablo Brener, Mexico City

37. *Sunday in Chapultepec.* 1934. Gouache, 10 × 12¾″. Collection Pablo Brener, Mexico City

38. *Women of Oaxaca.* 1938.
Watercolor, 18 × 13½″.
Collection Pablo Brener,
Mexico City

39. *Bowl of Fruit with Watermelon.* 1941. $16\frac{1}{2} \times 21\frac{3}{4}''$. Collection Pierre Matisse, New York

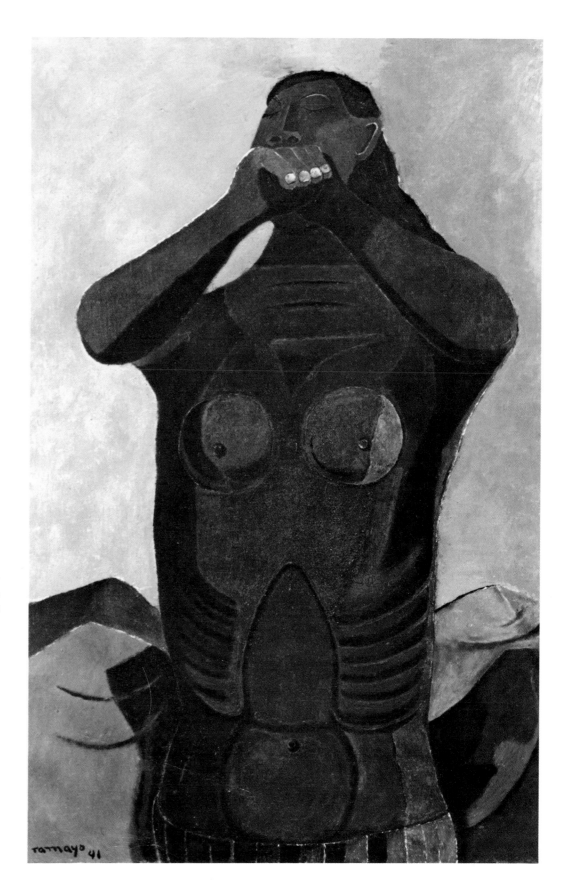

40. *Woman Calling.*
1941. 36 × 24".
Collection Lee Ault, New York

41. *Tortured Being.*
1949. $39\frac{3}{8} \times 31\frac{1}{2}''$.
Collection Sr. and Sra. Marte R. Gomez,
Mexico City

42. *Sleeping Musicians.* 1950. $53\frac{1}{8} \times 76\frac{3}{4}$". Museum of Modern Art, Mexico City

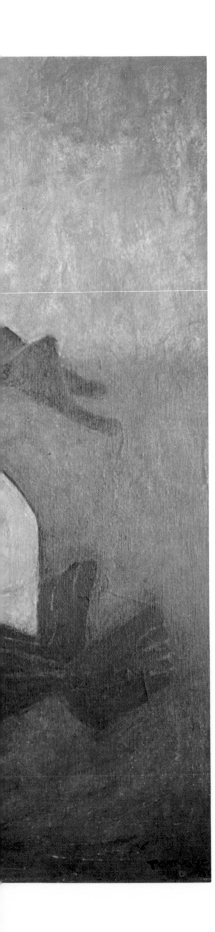

43. *Stargazer.* 1956. $39\frac{3}{8} \times 31\frac{1}{2}''$.
Private collection, Paris

44. *Woman Laughing.*
1950. $39\frac{3}{8} \times 31\frac{1}{2}''$.
E. B. Crocker Art Gallery,
Sacramento, Calif.

45. *Man*. 1953.
Vinyl with pigment
on vinyl white lead ground, mural.
Dallas Museum of Fine Arts

46. *Toast to Rejoicing.*
1956. $38\frac{1}{8} \times 31\frac{1}{2}''$.
Collection Dr. and Mrs. Jaime P. Constantiner,
Mexico City

47. *Supersonic Plane.* 1956. 21½ × 31″. Collection Dr. and Mrs. Jaime P. Constantiner, Mexico City

48. *Claustrophobia.* 1957. 32 × 39¼″. Collection Pablo Brener, Mexico City

49. *Figure*. 1957. $39\frac{1}{2} \times 31\frac{1}{2}''$.
Collection Pablo Brener,
Mexico City

50. *Three Personages in Black.* 1959. $37\frac{3}{8} \times 53\frac{1}{8}$". Private collection, Oslo, Norway

51. *Woman in Grey*. 1959. 76¾ × 53⅛″. Solomon R. Guggenheim Museum, New York

52. *Blue Bird.* 1960. $38\frac{1}{8} \times 51\frac{1}{8}''$. Private collection

53. *The Painter.*
1960. $38\frac{1}{8} \times 51\frac{1}{8}''$.
Collection
Mr. and Mrs. Raymond A. Young,
Oklahoma City

54. *Personages at Play.*
1960. $51\frac{1}{8} \times 76\frac{3}{4}''$.
Private collection, Paris

55. *Woman in Front of Mirror.*
1960. 37 × 29½″.
Private collection

56. *Man at the Door.*
1960. 76¾ × 51⅛″.
Collection
Sra. Marti Suneson, Mexico

58. *Dialogue at the Window.*
1961. $38\frac{1}{8} \times 51\frac{1}{8}''$.
Collection Olga Tamayo, Mexico City

59. *Man Before Picture*. 1961. 18$\frac{1}{8}$ × 21$\frac{5}{8}$″. Private collection

60.   *Shadow of a Man.* 1961. $31\frac{1}{2} \times 39\frac{3}{8}''$. Private collection, Rome

61. *Man*. 1961. $28\frac{3}{4} \times 36\frac{5}{8}''$. Collection Sra. Marti Suneson, Mexico

62. *Red Figure*. 1961. 18 × 21¾″. Collection Pablo Brener, Mexico City

63. *Composition with Two Figures.*
1962. $39\frac{3}{8} \times 31\frac{1}{2}''$.
Private collection

64. *Personages.* 1962.
$36\frac{5}{8} \times 26\frac{3}{4}''$.
Collection Roberto García Mora, Mexico

65. *Two Men*. 1962.
$39\frac{3}{8} \times 31\frac{1}{2}''$.
Private collection

67. *Man at the Door.*
1962. $39\frac{3}{8} \times 31\frac{1}{2}''$.
Museum of Modern Art,
Mexico City

66.   *Two Figures.*
1962. $39\frac{3}{8} \times 31\frac{1}{2}''$.
Private collection

68. *Afternoon Sun*. 1962. $31\frac{1}{2} \times 39\frac{3}{8}''$. Collection Ing. Enrique Anhalt, Mexico

69. *Still Life*. 1962. 18⅛ × 21⅝″. Collection Robert L. Cohen, Englewood, Colo.

70. *Boy at Window.* 1963. 19 × 26″. Collection Bernard Lewin, Beverly Hills

71. *Figures in White.*
1964. $39\frac{3}{8} \times 31\frac{1}{2}''$.
Private collection, Mexico City

72. *Man with the Red Sombrero.*
1963. $53\frac{1}{8} \times 37\frac{3}{8}''$.
Collection the artist

73. *Black Venus.*
1965. $39\frac{3}{8} \times 31\frac{1}{2}''$.
McElhenney Collection,
Austin, Tex.

74. *Man*. 1965.
$76\frac{3}{4} \times 53\frac{1}{2}''$.
Private collection

76. *Man with a Globe.*
1965. $31\frac{1}{2} \times 39\frac{3}{8}''$.
Private collection

75. *The Smoker.*
1965. $31\frac{1}{2} \times 26\frac{3}{8}''$.
Collection Angel Cespedes Rul,
Mexico City

77. *Ball Player.* 1965.
$31\frac{1}{2} \times 39\frac{3}{8}''$.
Private collection

78. *Couple.* 1965. $39\frac{3}{8} \times 31\frac{1}{2}''$.
Collection Mr. and Mrs. Eli Klein, Mexico City

79. *Persons Viewing an Eclipse.*
1965. $39\frac{3}{8} \times 31\frac{1}{2}''$. Private collection

80. *Man with Stick.* 1965. $39\frac{3}{8} \times 31\frac{1}{2}''$.
Collection Roberto García Mora, Mexico

81. *Family Portrait*. 1965. $37\frac{3}{8} \times 53\frac{1}{8}''$. Private collection

82. *Dancers.* 1965. $38\frac{1}{8} \times 51\frac{1}{8}''$. Private collection

83. *Two Children*. 1966. $37\frac{3}{8} \times 53\frac{1}{8}''$. Collection Mayalen Zunzunegui, Mexico

84. *Two Figures.*
1966. $39\frac{3}{8} \times 31\frac{1}{2}''$.
Private collection

85. *Three Women*. 1966. $53\frac{1}{8} \times 76\frac{3}{4}''$.
Collection Dr. and Mrs. Jaime P. Constantiner,
Mexico City

86. *Two Heads*. 1966.
Private collection

87. *Woman.* 1966.
$53\frac{1}{8} \times 37\frac{3}{8}''$.
Private collection, Mexico City

88. *Heads in White*. 1966. Private collection

89. *Torsos*. 1968.
$37\frac{3}{8} \times 53\frac{1}{8}''$.
Perls Galleries, New York

90. *Couple in the Garden*.
1966. $53\frac{1}{8} \times 76\frac{3}{4}''$.
Private collection, Mexico City

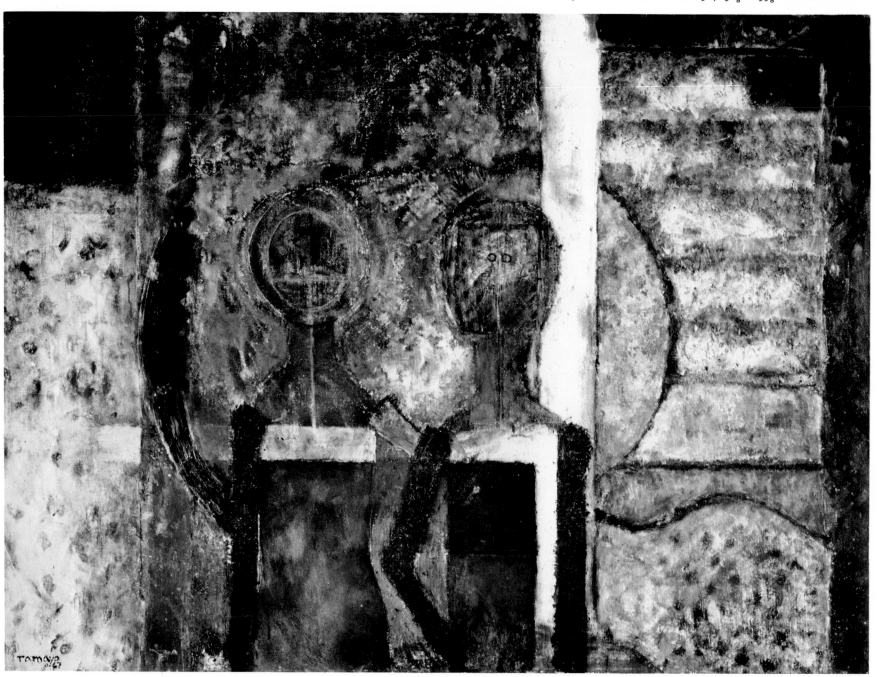

93. *Man and His Shadow*.
1968. 77 × 51″.
Private collection

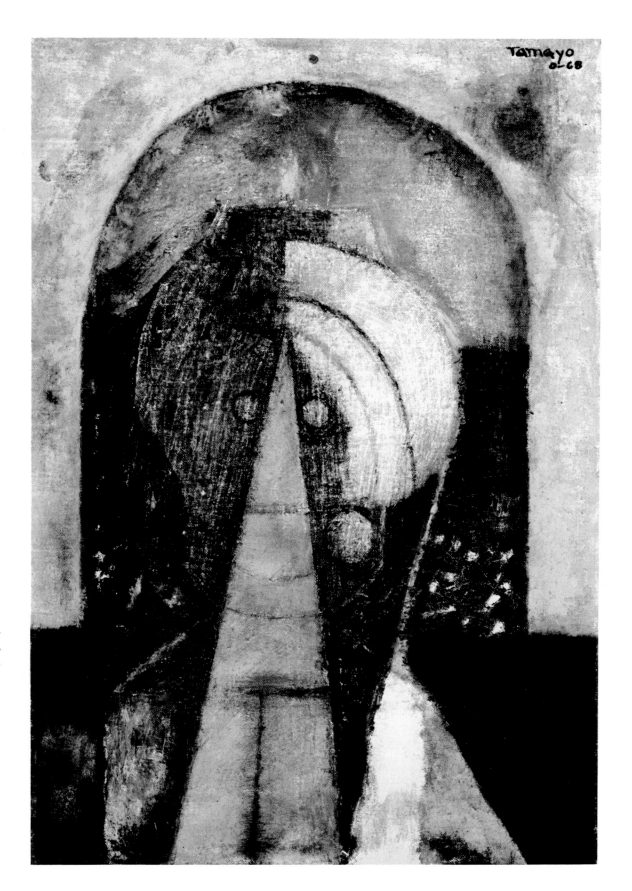

94. *Head.* 1968. 20 × 14″.
Collection Mr. and Mrs. Orme Lewis,
Scottsdale, Ariz.

95. *Two Women*. 1968.
$53\frac{1}{8} \times 38\frac{1}{8}''$.
Collection Anthony Quinn,
Bel Air, Calif.

97. *The Window*. 1968.
$53\frac{1}{8} \times 37\frac{3}{8}''$.
Collection John C. Sigurney,
Carmel Valley, Calif.

98. *Personage.* 1968. 31½ × 40″. Collection Bernard Lewin, Beverly Hills

99. *The Devil.* 1968. $37\frac{3}{8} \times 53\frac{1}{8}''$. Private collection

100. *Torso of a Man.*
1969. $39\frac{3}{8} \times 31\frac{1}{2}''$.
Collection
Emily Genauer Gash,
New York

101. *Man in Red.* 1969.
$39\frac{3}{8} \times 31\frac{1}{2}''$.
Collection Bernard Lewin,
Beverly Hills

102. *Dynamic Torso.* 1969.
$39\frac{3}{8} \times 31\frac{1}{2}''$.
Collection Luis Arzae, Mexico

103. *A Man and a Woman.*
1969. $39\frac{3}{8} \times 31\frac{1}{2}''$.
Private collection, Mexico

104. *Three Figures.* 1969.
$39\frac{3}{8} \times 31\frac{1}{2}''$.
Perls Galleries, New York

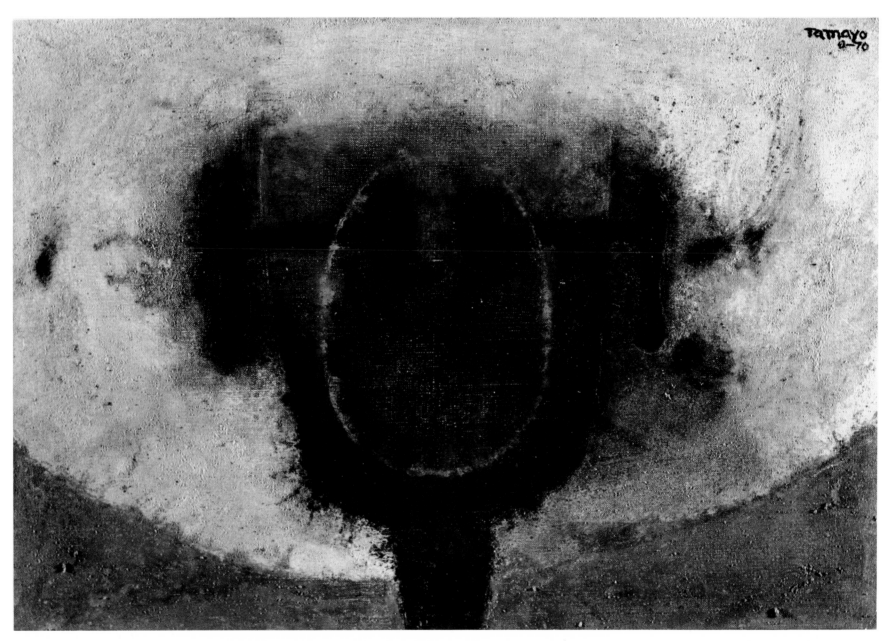

106.   *Head with Red.* 1970. 13⅞ × 19¾″. Private collection, Phoenix

107. *Personage in Black.* 1970. $31\frac{1}{2} \times 39\frac{3}{8}''$. Collection Alexander Calder

108. *Man and Woman.* 1970.
$76\frac{3}{4} \times 53\frac{1}{8}''$.
Private collection, Phoenix

109. *The Solitary.* 1970.
$53\frac{1}{8} \times 37\frac{3}{8}''$.
Perls Galleries, New York

110. *Two Figures and the Moon.*
1970. $39\frac{3}{8} \times 31\frac{1}{2}''$.
Private collection

III. *Two Women in Space.* 1970.
$53\frac{1}{8} \times 37\frac{3}{8}''$.
Collection Steve Jacobson,
New York

112.   *Three Personages No. 2.* 1970. 37⅜ × 53⅛″. Collection Steve Jacobson, New York

114. *Dialogue.* 1971. $38\frac{1}{4} \times 51\frac{1}{4}$". Private collection

115. *Man and Woman.* 1971.
$31\frac{1}{2} \times 27\frac{5}{8}''$.
Collection
Mr. and Mrs. Norton S. Walbridge,
Calif.

116. *Head.* 1971.
$13\frac{3}{4} \times 7\frac{7}{8}''$.
Collection Vera Neumann,
New York

117.   *Couple in Black*. 1971. $53\frac{1}{8} \times 76\frac{3}{4}''$. Collection the artist

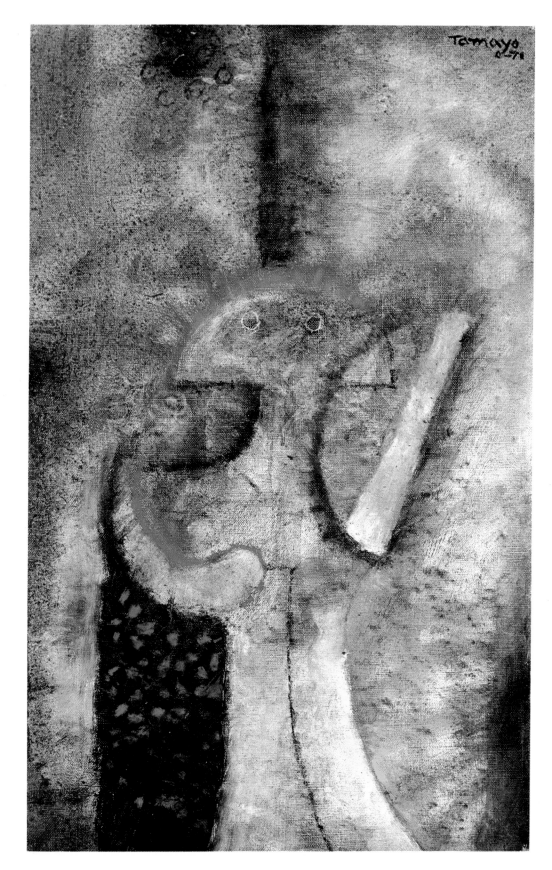

118. *Figure in Movement.* 1971.
$15\frac{3}{4} \times 9\frac{7}{8}''$.
Collection Michael Barr, New York

119. *Men in Space.* 1971.
$39\frac{3}{8} \times 31\frac{1}{2}''$.
Perls Galleries, New York

120. *Man and His Shadow.* 1971.
$19\frac{5}{8} \times 15\frac{3}{4}''$.
Private collection

121. *Personage.* 1971.
$13\frac{3}{4} \times 7\frac{7}{8}''$.
Perls Galleries, New York

122. *Image in the Mirror.*
1972. $39\frac{3}{8} \times 31\frac{1}{2}''$.
Collection the artist

123. *Dialogue.* 1972.
$39\frac{3}{8} \times 31\frac{1}{2}''$.
Collection the artist

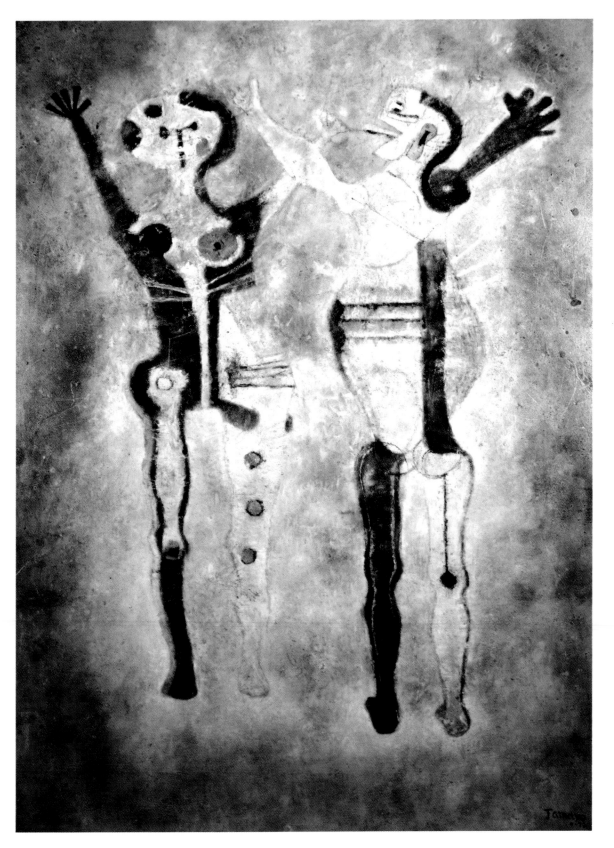

124. *Struggle.* 1972.
51 × 38″.
Perls Galleries, New York

125. *Hippie.* 1972. 51 × 38″.
Perls Galleries, New York

126. *Fishmongers.* 1972. $37\frac{1}{2} \times 53\frac{1}{8}''$. Collection the artist

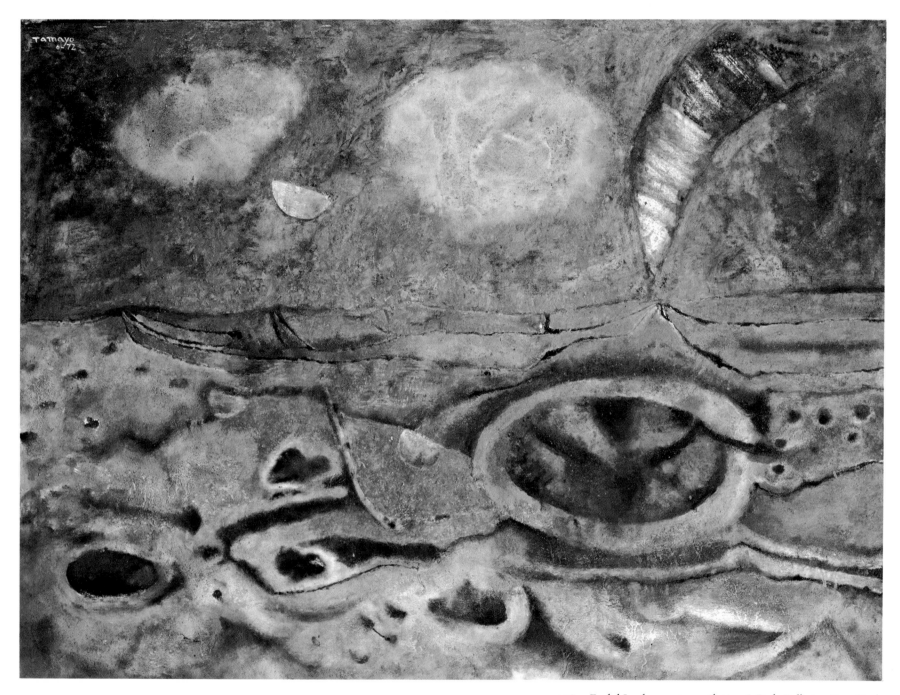

128. *Eroded Landscape.* 1972. $38\frac{1}{4} \times 51''$. Perls Galleries, New York

129. *Arid Landscape.* 1973. $38\frac{1}{8} \times 51\frac{1}{8}''$. Perls Galleries, New York

130. *Study in Blue and Brown.*
1973. $56\frac{7}{8} \times 43''$.
Harry N. Abrams Family Collection

131. *Commemorative Bust.* 1973. 43 × 58⅞″. Collection Mr. and Mrs. Lee Ault, New York

BIOGRAPHICAL OUTLINE

1899 Born of Zapotec Indian parents in Oaxaca, Mexico.

1911 After the death of his parents, goes to Mexico City to live with aunt. Attends school and helps aunt in her fruit market.

1915 Aunt, hoping he will someday assist in the –16 management of her market, sends him to commercial school. Secretly studies drawing in night classes.

1917 Studies at the San Carlos Academy of Fine –21 Arts in Mexico City.

1921 Leaves the San Carlos Academy, disappointed with its conservative program, to paint alone. Is appointed head of the Department of Ethnographic Drawing at the National Museum of Archaeology, Mexico City. At intervals during early 1920s, teaches in primary schools of Mexico City and in the program of open air, rural schools established by Minister of Education José Vasconcelos.

1926 Has first one-man show in small shop on Avenida Madero in Mexico City. Visits New York with friend, composer Carlos Chávez; they decide to remain in New York. Exhibition at Weyhe Gallery.

1928 Because of illness, returns to Mexico City. Begins teaching at the National School of Fine Arts.

1929 Exhibitions at the National Theater (now Palace of Fine Arts) and the Galería de Arte Moderno in Mexico City.

1930 Leaves National School of Fine Arts after disagreeing with both Communists and aesthetic conservatives.

1931 Represents painters on four-man Council for the Fine Arts in the Ministry of Education. Exhibition at the John Levy Gallery, New York.

1932 Is appointed head of the Department of Plastic Arts, Ministry of Education, Mexico City.

1933 Paints mural on the theme of music for the National School of Music, Mexico City.

1934 Marries Olga Flores Rivas, also a native of Oaxaca.

133. Tamayo in Mexico City, 1934

134. Tamayo in New York, 1942

135. Rufino and Olga Tamayo
with Frederick and Emily Genauer Gash at
Xochimilco Gardens, Mexico City, 1945

136. Rufino and Olga Tamayo
leaving Paris for New York, 1950

1935   Exhibitions at the Galería de Arte Mexicano and the Galería de Carolina Amor in Mexico City.

1936   Attends Artists' Congress in New York as a delegate of the Mexican League of Revolutionary Painters and Artists. Moves to New York where he will live intermittently for over 18 years.

1937   Exhibitions at the Julien Levy Gallery in New York and the Howard Putzel Gallery in San Francisco.

1938   Paints mural for the National Museum of Anthropology, Mexico City. Begins teaching at the Dalton School, New York.

1939   Exhibition at the Valentine Gallery, New York.

1940   Exhibition at the Valentine Gallery, New York. Is represented in the exhibition "20 Centuries of Mexican Art" at the Museum of Modern Art, New York.

1942   Exhibition at the Valentine Gallery, New York.

1943   Paints mural *Nature and the Artist* for the Hillyer Art Library, Smith College, Northampton, Mass. Contributes several paintings to the exhibition "Mexican Art Today" at the Philadelphia Museum of Art.

1944   Exhibition at the Galería de Arte Mexicano, Mexico City.

137.   Tamayo in his New York studio, 1950

1945   Exhibition at the Arts Club of Chicago. Is represented in show of "Eleven 20th Century Nudes" at the Pierre Matisse Gallery, New York.

1946   Is appointed Instructor at the Brooklyn Museum Art School where he teaches the Tamayo workshop. Exhibition at the Valentine Gallery, New York.

1947   First monograph on Tamayo is published by Robert Goldwater (Quadrangle Press, New York). Exhibitions at the Modern Art Society of the Cincinnati Art Museum, the Valentine Gallery and the Pierre Matisse Gallery in New York, and the Galería de Arte Mexicano in Mexico City.

1948   Is honored on his 25th anniversary as a painter with a retrospective show at the Palace of Fine Arts, Mexico City.

1949   Makes first trip to Europe and remains in Paris. Exhibition at the Galería Central de Arte Misrachi, Mexico City.

1950   Has one-man show of 16 paintings in room dedicated to him at the Biennale, Venice. Exhibitions at the Galerie des Beaux-Arts, Paris; the Palais des Beaux-Arts, Brussels; and M. Knoedler & Co., New York.

1951   Exhibitions at the Instituto de Arte Moderno, Buenos Aires; the Salón de la Plástica Mexicana, Mexico City; the Frank Perls Gallery, Los Angeles; and M. Knoedler & Co., New York.

1952   Is awarded Third Prize at the Carnegie International Exhibition, Pittsburgh. Executes mural *The Birth of Nationality* for the Palace of Fine Arts, Mexico City. Participates in exhibition "Art Mexicain du Précolumbien à nos jours" at the Musée National d'Art Moderne in Paris. Exhibitions at the Fort Worth Art Museum and the Pan American Union, Washington, D.C.

1953   Shares Grand Prize for Painting at the Bienal, São Paulo, Brazil, with Alfred Manessier of France. Executes mural *Mexico Today* for the Palace of Fine Arts, Mexico City, and mural *Man* for the Dallas Museum of Fine Arts. Exhibitions at the Galerías Excélsior and the Salón de la Plástica in Mexico City; M. Knoedler & Co., New York; the Frank Perls Gallery, Los Angeles; the Santa Barbara Museum of Art; and the San Francisco Museum of Art.

1954   Executes mural for Sanborn's in Mexico City.

1955   Is awarded Second Prize at the Carnegie International Exhibition, Pittsburgh. Executes

138. Tamayo with students of the University of Puerto Rico, San Juan, 1957

139. Tamayo and Henry Moore in Xochicalco, 1959

140. Rufino and Olga Tamayo with Manolo Ortiz in Cordoba, Spain, 1960

mural *America* for the Bank of the Southwest, Houston. Exhibition at the Main Street Gallery, Chicago.

1956 Exhibitions at the Galería Antonio Souza, Mexico City; the Museum of Fine Arts, Houston; and M. Knoedler & Co., New York.

1957 Is made a Chevalier de la Légion d'Honneur. Executes mural *Prometheus* for the Library of the University of Puerto Rico, San Juan.

1958 Executes mural *Prometheus Bringing Fire to Man* for the Conference Room of the UNESCO Building, Paris. Exhibitions at the Galerie de France, Paris, and the Galleria del Milione, Milan.

1959 Is elected Member of the Academy of Arts, Buenos Aires. Participates in international exhibition "Documenta II" in Kassel, Germany. Exhibitions at the Kunstnerns Hus, Oslo; the Felix Landau Galleries, Los Angeles; and M. Knoedler & Co., New York.

1960 Is awarded Guggenheim International Foundation Prize. Exhibitions at the Galerie de France, Paris, and the New Art Center Gallery, New York.

1961 Is elected Honorary Member of the American Academy of Arts and Letters of the United States.

1962 Exhibitions at the Galería de Arte Misrachi, Mexico City, and M. Knoedler & Co., New York.

1963 Circulating exhibition organized by the Museums Association of Israel. Executes murals *Israel Yesterday* and *Israel Today* for the Israeli ocean liner "Shalom." Retrospective exhibition of 71 works organized by the Mainichi Newspapers, Tokyo.

1964 Is awarded the Premio Nacional by the

141. Tamayo with his portrait
of his wife, Olga, 1962

142. Rufino and Olga Tamayo
in Mexico, 1969

143. Tamayo working in his
Mexico City studio, 1971

President of Mexico. At the invitation of the Ford Foundation, executes 26 lithographs, each in an edition of 20, at the Tamarind Workshop, Los Angeles. Executes mural *Duality* for the National Museum of Anthropology, Mexico City.

1965 Exhibition at the Galerie Semiha Huber, Zurich.

1966 Executes mural *San Cristobal* for the offices of Sr. Roberto García Mora, Mexico City. Exhibition at the Galería de Arte Misrachi, Mexico City.

1967 Executes mural for the Mexican Pavilion at "Expo '67," Montreal.

1968 Is honored on his fiftieth anniversary as a painter with a retrospective exhibition of 103 paintings and lithographs at the Palace of Fine Arts, Mexico City. Exhibition of 124 works from American collections at the Phoenix Art Museum. Is Honor Guest of the Venice Biennale where he is accorded an exhibition of 70 paintings. Executes mural for the Mexican Pavilion at Hemisfair, San Antonio.

1969 Creates 20 lithographs at the Atelier Desjaubert of Paris for Touchstone and Co., New York. Executes mural *Energy* at the Industrial Club of Mexico, Mexico City. Is awarded the Ibico Reggino Prize of Reggio Calabria, Italy, by the President of Italy and the Calouste Gulbenkian Award by the Institut de France, Paris.

1970 Is elected Officier de la Légion d'Honneur.

1971 Is elected Commendatore de la Repubblica Italiana. Executes mural *Man Confronting Infinity* for the Camino Real Hotel, Mexico City; it is dedicated by the President of Mexico. Exhibition at the Perls Galleries, New York.

144. Tamayo at the entrance to
the Museum of
Pre-Spanish Mexican Art, Oaxaca, 1974

145. Tamayo in the courtyard
of the Museum of Pre-Spanish Mexican Art,
Oaxaca, 1974

146. Tamayo with part of
the sculpture collection at the Museum of
Pre-Spanish Mexican Art, Oaxaca, 1974

1972 Is invited by the Government to visit the People's Republic of China. Work is begun in Oaxaca on museum to house his Pre-Columbian collection. Mexican government purchases Olga Tamayo's collection of 30 Tamayo paintings.

1973 Visits Spain, where he executes 15 lithographs for Poligrafa editions in Barcelona, and Italy, where he executes 6 lithographs for

editor Giorgio Alessandrini in Rome. Exhibitions at the Galería de Arte Misrachi, Mexico City, and the Perls Galleries, New York.

1974 The Museum of Pre-Spanish Mexican Art opens in Oaxaca. The Museum and its collection of 2,000 pre-Spanish ceramics and sculptures are the gift of Tamayo to the people of Oaxaca.

SELECTED BIBLIOGRAPHY

BOOKS

Alba, Víctor. *Coloquios de Coyoacán con Rufino Tamayo.* Mexico City: B. Costa-Amic, 1956 (originally in *Panoramas*, no. 3, pt. 5, 1956, pp. 199–278).

Barreda, Octavio G. *Thirteen Mexican Painters.* Mexico City: José Segu, 1940s.

Cardoza y Aragón, Luis. "Rufino Tamayo" in *La nube y el reloj.* Mexico City: Universidad Nacional Autónoma, 1940.

———. *Rufino Tamayo.* Text in Spanish, English, and French. Mexico City: Palacio de Bellas Artes, 1934.

Cogniat, Raymond. *Rufino Tamayo.* Paris: Presses Littéraires de France, 1951.

Edwards, Emily, and Bravo, M. Alvarez. "The Mural Revolution" in *Painted Walls of Mexico: From Prehistoric Times Until Today.* Austin: University of Texas Press, 1966.

Fernández, Justino. *Rufino Tamayo.* Mexico City: Imprenta Universitaria, 1948.

Goldwater, Robert. *Rufino Tamayo.* New York: The Quadrangle Press, 1947.

Gual, Enrique. *Dibujos de Tamayo.* Issued in portfolio. Spanish text with English insert. Mexico City: Ediciones Mexicanas, S. A., 1949.

———. *Rufino Tamayo.* Mexico City: Editorial Eugenio Fishgrund, 1950.

Helm, McKinley. *Modern Mexican Painters.* New York and London: Harper and Brothers, 1941.

Myers, Bernard S. *Mexican Painting in Our Time.* New York: Oxford University Press, 1956.

Mural Painting of the Mexican Revolution, 1921–60. Introduction by Carlos Pellicer. Mexico City: Fondo Editorial de la Plástica Mexicana, 1960.

Palencia, Ceferino. *Rufino Tamayo.* Mexico City: Ediciones de Arte, S. A., 1950.

Paz, Octavio. *Tamayo en la Pintura Mexicana.* Text in Spanish, English, and French. Trans. by Sita Garst. Mexico City: Universidad Nacional Autónoma de México, 1959.

Ponce, Juan García. *Tamayo.* Trans. by Emma Gutiérrez Suarez. Mexico City: Galería de Arte Misrachi and New York: Tudor Publishing Co., 1967.

Reed, Alma M. *The Mexican Muralists.* New York: Crown, 1960.

Rodman, Selden. *Mexican Journal: The Conquerors Conquered.* Includes an interview with Tamayo. New York: Devin-Adair, 1958.

Rodríguez, Antonio. "Tamayo: Another Kind of Mexican" in *A History of Mexican Mural Painting.* Trans. by Marina Corby. New York: Putnam, 1969.

Tamayo, Rufino. *Air mexicain.* Portfolio of lithographs. Introduction by Benjamin Péret. Paris: Librairie Arcanes, 1952.

——. *Tamayo*. Fifteen reproductions in portfolio. Introduction by Octavio Paz. Mexico City: Instituto Nacional de Bellas Artes, 1967.

Villaurrutia, Xavier. *Rufino Tamayo*. Buenos Aires: Instituto de Arte Moderno, 1951.

Westheim, Paul. *Tamayo: A Study in Esthetics*. Trans. by Mariana Frenk. Mexico City: Artes de México, 1957.

Zabludovsky, Jacobo. *Charlos con pintores*. Introduction by David Alfaro Siqueiros. Mexico City: B. Costa-Amic, 1966.

ARTICLES

Breton, André. "L'Europe découvre Rufino Tamayo," *Arts-Documents*, January, 1951, pp. 8–9.

Burchard, J. E. "UNESCO House Appraised," *Architectural Record*, vol. 127, May, 1960, pp. 152–55.

Cardoza y Aragón, Luis. "Rufino Tamayo; un nuevo ciclo de la pintura de México," *Cuadernos americanos*, vol. 40, July-August, 1948, pp. 250–60.

Cassou, Jean. "Les Arts plastiques au nouveau siège de l'UNESCO: Tamayo: Prométhée apportant le feu aux hommes," *Quadrum*, vol. 6, 1959, pp. 23–25.

Charlot, Jean. "Rufino Tamayo: One of the Murals in the Hillyer Art Library," *Magazine of Art*, Smith College, vol. 38, April, 1945, pp. 138–45.

Genauer, Emily. "Liberation of Mexican Mural Art Hailed as Tamayo Completes Panel," *New York Herald Tribune*, October 5, 1952.

——. "Mexico City's Modern Mayan," *New York Herald Tribune*, September 20, 1953.

——. "Tamayo at the Valentine," *New York World Telegram*, February 4, 1939.

Gonzales y Contreras, Gilberto. "Rufino Tamayo," *Arquitectura*, no. 27, April, 1949, pp. 113–17.

——. "Rufino Tamayo," *Espacios*, September, 1948.

Hunter, Sam. "Tamayo: Fire and Ice," *Art Digest*, vol. 28, March 15, 1954, pp. 17, 32–33.

Joysmith, Toby. "Two Magic Worlds of Rufino Tamayo," *Artist's Proof*, vol. 7, 1967, pp. 40–43.

Lewis, Flora. "Mexican Counter-Revolt: Artist Tamayo Doing Official Murals in Mexico City, Claims Victory over 'Social Message' School of Art," *The New York Times*, October 12, 1952.

MacBride, Henry. "Rufino Tamayo Here Comments on His Art," *St. Louis Post-Dispatch*, November 12, 1948.

"Mr. Tamayo of Mexico," *Look*, vol. 15, September 25, 1951, pp. 106–10.

Montaño, Jorge. "Rufino Tamayo, Leader of a New Mexican School of Painting," *Mexican Life*, vol. 5, November, 1929, pp. 23–27.

Moreno Galván, J. M. "La pintura de Rufino Tamayo," *Goya*, no. 33, November-December, 1959, pp. 164–69.

Myers, Bernard S. "Tamayo Versus the Mexican Mural Painters," *College Art Journal*, vol. 13, Winter, 1954, pp. 101–5.

Parker, Howard. "Rufino Tamayo," *Mexican Folk-ways*, vol. 7, April-June, 1932, pp. 75–81.

Paz, Octavio. "Tamayo et la peinture mexicaine," *Cahiers du musée de peche*, no. 1, March, 1959, pp. 81–93.

Tamayo, Olga. "Una carta de la esposa de Rufino Tamayo," *Excélsior*, September 9, 1951.

Tamayo, Rufino. "A Statement" (with Spanish translation), *Smith College Museum Bulletin*, no. 24, October, 1943, pp. 4–13.

———. "Los frescos del Smith College," *Letras de México*, vol. 4, no. 15, 1944.

"Tamayo: After 15-Year Exile, Mexican Painter Wins Fame at Home," *Life*, vol. 34, March 16, 1953, pp. 98–105.

Trotta, Gerald. "Tamayo Paints a Picture: Lunatic," *Art News*, vol. 50, October, 1951, pp. 28–31, 67.

Westheim, Paul. "Segunda Bienal interamericana de México: 50 obras de Tamayo," *Artes de México*, vol. 6, no. 35, 1961, pp. 1–56 including 48 plates. Text in Spanish; English trans. by Maria Melgar.

Villaurrutia, Xavier. "Rufino Tamayo," *México en el Arte*, no. 2, August, 1948, pp. 37–54.

EXHIBITION CATALOGUES

Philadelphia. Philadelphia Museum of Art. "Mexican Art Today," 1943. Text in Spanish and English by Luis Cardoza y Aragón. Includes 5 Tamayo plates.

Mexico City. Instituto Nacional de Bellas Artes, Museo Nacional de Artes Plásticas. "Tamayo: 20 años de su labor pictorica," 1949. Text by Xavier Villaurrutia.

New York. M. Knoedler & Co. "Tamayo," April 24–May 13, 1950.

Paris. Galerie des Beaux-Arts. "Tamayo," November 8–December 9, 1950. Text by Jean Cassou and André Breton.

New York. M. Knoedler & Co., "Recent Works by Tamayo," November 19–December 15, 1951.

New York. M. Knoedler & Co. "Tamayo," February 24–March 20, 1954.

New York. M. Knoedler & Co. "Recent Works by Rufino Tamayo," October 30–November 17, 1956.

New York. M. Knoedler & Co. "Tamayo," November 17–December 12, 1959.

New York. M. Knoedler & Co. "Tamayo," May 15–June 9, 1962.

Phoenix. Phoenix Art Museum. "Tamayo," March, 1968. Commentary by the Artist and Introduction by James B. Lynch, Jr.

New York. Perls Galleries. "Rufino Tamayo: Oil Paintings, 1970–1971," November 9–December 11, 1971. Introduction by Klaus Perls.

New York. Perls Galleries. "Rufino Tamayo: Oil Paintings, 1972–1973," November 6–December 8, 1973. Introduction by Emily Genauer.

PHOTOGRAPHIC CREDITS